The big bubble

Per Grankvist

The big bubble

How technology makes it harder
to understand the world

About the author

PER GRANKVIST is a well-known journalist and author in Sweden, who has written on the impact of digital media and technology on politics and civic engagement in some of Sweden's largest newspapers. Drawing on science, psychology and history and his award-wining ability to make technology understandable, he makes technology feel a little less alien and a bit more human.

Although he has written four books and several essays in Swedish, this is his first book be translated in English. Mr. Grankvist lives and works in Stockholm, Sweden.

Introduction

Introduction   7

Part 1. – A digital reality   31
   Technology as an enabler   34
   Artificial intelligence   52
   Hasty conclusions   60
   The dangers of filter bubbles   70

Part 2. – A Personalized reality   89
   Media habits have changed   92
   The algorithm as editor   101
   The filter bubbles of journalists   108

Part 3. – A Faked reality   123
   The truth about fake news   132
   Fighting fake news   144
   with algorithms   144
   The importance of   152
   understanding how media works   152
   Something's not quite right   161
   The crisis of faith in institutions 170
   Five ways to change your bubble   183

Acknowledgements   201
Endnotes   205

Introduction

Being well-informed is especially important if you have the power to unleash fire and fury upon another nation with the intent of totally destroy that nation. Which is why the President of the United States is receiving a daily brief containing important and classified documents, early each morning, irrespective of where in the world he might be. One of the folders included in the daily brief contains the latest analysis of issues related to national security and global conflicts from the Office of the Director of National Intelligence. Another folder contains documents with background information on the day's meetings, who is to be involved, and any topics likely to be raised. A third folder contains a summary of public opinion and press clippings exemplifying how the President and the agenda he is pursuing are currently being portrayed in the media. The purpose of these folders is to offer the President a complete overview of the situation at home and abroad, based on robust documentation, so that he or she is able to make balanced decisions with the nation's best interests at heart.

Naturally, different presidents have had varying wishes as to what should be included in the brief and how often it should be presented. John F. Kennedy preferred a concise briefing in a format that allowed him to carry the most essential information in the inner pocket of his jacket. George W. Bush did not want to be briefed on Sundays. Barack Obama liked to receive all folders and information digitally. Donald Trump has his own opinions about the content of the briefing folders itself. He only wants positive news.

White House staff is, therefore, tasked with sorting through the media stream to identify the most positive news reports on the President and his policies. Their task is to find 20-30 items, twice a day. The content is a mixture of positive assessments from TV morning show hosts, admiring tweets, articles reprinting favorable quotes about the President from people on the street, appreciative social media posts, homages in the conservative or right-wing press, and the occasional image of Mr. Trump looking imposing in a television appearance. On days when positive news is thin on the ground, staff in charge of putting together the folder have been known to wander the White House in search of favorable images of the President for inclusion in what is known internally as "the propaganda folder."[1] The purpose of the folder is to keep the famously ill-tempered and egocentric President in good spirits by enabling him to maintain a distorted image of himself and the world.

How do you go about obtaining a correct image of the world? One way is to follow public discourse to see what various pundits think about current events. If you're like me, this means that you read the newspapers or use a news app on your phone. You may scroll through what people are saying on Twitter or your feed on Facebook.

Listening to the arguments of both sides in a debate is however not the same as understanding what is true and what's not. If person A claim climate change is man-made and person B claims it is not, the truth is not somewhere in between. Besides that, what you're getting in your feed might only be voices that sound like person B, declaring that the talk of climate change is exaggerated or that it's all a conspiracy by the left.

During an election campaign, the difficulty in getting an objective view of the word is particularly demanding. Partisan news and targeted ads only confirm what supporters of a particular candidate or political party already believe to be true and reinforce their biases of their opponents. All sides seem to convey an image "of the other side" as a group of people that is always providing an exaggerated or false view of reality.

One used to be able to rely on media to get an objective view of the world. Being impartial is what journalism is supposed to be about. Even if some media chose to lean to the left and others to the right, they would share the same basic approach to the craft. An editor might choose to tell a story from a particular angle, but they would remain impartial doing so in order to avoid being seen as a propaganda tool for one party. Impartiality is a basic tenet of journalism. There are media outlets that occupy a position more to the right or left in their attitudes to the world and to power, but they still share the same basic approach to their craft. Even if the editor chooses a certain angle to a news story, they will attempt to avoid picking sides, being perceived as biased, or appearing to propagandize for one point of view or the other. Truthfulness, accuracy, objectivity, impartiality, fairness and public accountability has been part of the journalistic creed for more than a century.

The opinions of both sides in a conflict should be reported and the reader/listener/viewer should always be able to trust the facts. By comparing how different media outlets report an event, you can also see whether a news story is true (several reports independently stating the same basic facts) and obtain a somewhat more in-depth understanding of what has occurred (thanks to the various angles the outlets have chosen to adopt).

At least, that's what it used to be like.

Over the course of a few decades the public trust in media has slowly deteriorated. Accusations of media withholding information or refraining from reporting some news as a result of political motives have become more common in recent years. Some media outlets have even been publicly accused of publishing things news that are completely made up in order to help one party advance their political agenda. For the average reader, listener or viewer it's not easy to discern whether a new story is correct. Some guidance is available, such as giving due consideration to who has published the story. To complicate things, news may be published on websites that appear confusingly similar to highly reliable news sources but which are actually faked for the sole purpose of fooling visitors into believing one thing or another, and then disseminating it.

One method of checking the facts, in the past and theory at least, is by using an encyclopedia. Nowadays, we "google" instead. Search engines, as we all know, work quite differently from an encyclopedia. The results displayed when you search are not sorted based on their veracity, but rather on their relevance. Or more precisely, what others searching for the same thing consider relevant. If the question is a simple one, such as who is the current President of the United States, the answer will generally be correct. If the question is more complicated, such as whether or not Donald Trump is considered to be a good president, there will seldom be a uniform answer, which makes it difficult to check whether something is true or false. In addition, it is often said that Google adapts its search results to the individual user, making the work of fact-finding even harder as the answer depends on who is asking.

If you are like me, and many others, you will obtain a great deal of your news via Facebook. Mixed with updates from friends and acquaintances, you will find links to the news that is currently engaging people the most. Once upon a time, Facebook was just one app among many on our phones. Today, it is a political and cultural force with worldwide influence and, for many people, the effects of this change first became apparent in conjunction with the US presidential election of 2016. When the companies that created the platforms we call "social media" talk about their users they are prone to rhetoric. Users are "members" and are described as being part of a digital "community."

When these companies first appeared, they promised to provide platforms unparalleled in human history. A forum where all stakeholders – citizens, politicians, media, NGOs (non-governmental organizations), and businesses alike – would be able to congregate and discuss the issues close to their hearts. In this new public sphere, the lonely were to find soulmates, engagement was to be born and flourish, all voices were to be heard and given the chance to participate in a common discussion about the things that mean something to them.

It felt like a new kind of freedom, and the social media platforms seemed to deliver what they promised, but, in reality, this was never anything but a commercial opportunity. Companies behaved like liberal thinkers and used language reminiscent of democratic institutions, despite the fact that they determined all of the rules. To behave like a quasi-state may sound cynical, but cynicism is not an adequate explanation for how the current state of affairs came to be. It is not a trait that I have come across particularly often among entrepreneurs during the almost twenty years I have been closely following the development of different digital services. It is, however, common to harbor a naive belief in the digitalization of society as solely a positive development for citizens. Of course, in many cases, users have proved to be equally starry-eyed. During the development phase of these privately-owned digital societies, the image of the platforms as tools enhancing democracy has served corporations well. It is easier for users to share large parts of their private lives with a business that lives by capitalizing their users' data if they believe that the company is somehow something more. As these large online platforms have grown, thereby influencing an ever-increasing proportion of the public sphere, their influence over that sphere – both positive and negative – has become more obvious.

Nowadays, it is meaningless to divide reality into the physical and the virtual. The digitalization of everyday processes has fused these together. Atoms and bits occur helter-skelter. Digitalization has resulted in what was once static becoming elastic, often adapted to whoever is using it. The intention is good. The optimistic view of the effects is often extremely naive. As an example, it sounds handy that news services customize and filter content based on user preferences, but the effect is simultaneously to reduce our ability to mentally collate a folder of news clippings when we want to obtain a true picture of reality. Like it or not, technology is making it harder to understand the world as it creates a big bubble around us.

This book is an attempt to map how manipulative algorithms, constrictive filter bubbles, and fake news have made it harder than ever to cut through the crap and gain a well-founded factual understanding of the times in which we live. However, it is not impossible.

This book will help you decode the digital media we take for granted, beginning at the source. By understanding the logic that structures the source code, that controls the algorithm that creates the filter bubbles that seem to make it so difficult for us to separate fake news from real. By understanding how media are engineered, we can also learn how they engineer our worldview and, thus, how we can act to counteract their intrusion, for example, by learning the basics of source evaluation.

In the final part of the book, I have summarized some of the options available to cut through the static, construct an accurate worldview, and avoid becoming trapped in a bubble.

Algorithms, filter bubbles, and fake news

In order to obtain new knowledge, we must trust in others who know more. Human knowledge is essentially social. This means that the more people we have contact with, the more likely we are to obtain new knowledge. From a historical perspective, people in general have always benefited from as many people as possible having a forum to share their knowledge. The flipside of the democratization of the public sphere that the Internet has contributed to is that it becomes difficult to decide who has useful knowledge and who is pedaling falsehoods, whether accidentally or deliberately.

In order to assist their users in navigating the broad but fragmented information stream, Facebook, Instagram, Twitter, and many other companies use algorithms. Algorithm is simply a fancy way of describing an equation that takes into consideration a number of factors in order to present a certain result. When you look at your Facebook feed, you will find posts from friends that appear to be random. However, their composition is actually a selection made by an algorithm, an algorithm that guesses which of all of your friends' posts are the most relevant to you and prioritizes the order of that information. Many news sites do exactly the same thing, adapting their front pages to the preferences of the visitor. Algorithms have learned that I have little or no interest in sports (I never click on links to sports-related articles) and, therefore, sports news is rarely shown in my feed. I do, however, occasionally see articles linked to horse show jumping, as I have a friend who is an accomplished equestrian, and I obviously read articles about him. Another parameter is that social media algorithms prioritize posts linked to those we have close social relationships with.

In their haste to compile feeds that are as relevant as possible, algorithms filter out everything we appear to dislike until we are surrounded solely by things we will in all likelihood enjoy and want to read. This is true for topics as well as for sources. If you read the New York Times, you will see more articles from that source versus other sources (such as Fox News). The effect is that we are left in a filter bubble in which we see only confirmation of what we already believe. In addition, this big bubble grows ever more constrictive over time as the algorithm, by showing us only things we like, reinforces its own assumptions about what it is we like and narrows results further. Everything else is filtered out. The result is an echo chamber in which only certain opinions resound.

To have knowledge implies the possession of information, facts and skills acquired by a person through experience or education that forms the basis of healthy, well-founded convictions on which we can base our worldview.

However, sometimes we fool ourselves. If we are convinced that something is true, we have a tendency to seek confirmation of our own beliefs. This phenomenon is called "confirmation bias" and has been recognized by psychologists for decades. Instead of exposing our convictions to critical review, we do all we can to confirm them, ignoring information that conflicts or challenges those convictions. Confirmation bias then, is the human equivalent of the algorithm and plays a central role in understanding people's ability to form an idea of the world – offering a direct parallel to the algorithm's ability to compile social media feeds. Thus, in social media, an unfortunate reinforcement effect arises when human confirmation bias meets algorithms' filtering and information prioritization. The effect is that it becomes *even more* difficult to construct an accurate view of reality.

Donald Trump has repeatedly used the term "fake news" whenever he hears something that doesn't fit with or challenges his view of the world. A folder in his morning brief containing nothing but positive news is a filter bubble in miniature that excludes all negativity. The effect is a well-developed immunity to facts (which in Mr. Trump's case began to develop long before he became president). It is, however, also an example of "politically motivated reasoning," to use Dan Kahan's term. Mr. Kahn is a professor of law and psychology at Yale Law School who, together with his colleagues, has studied our tendency to seek confirmation of the opinions associated with our own ideological and cultural group. Their research shows that, when an issue is politically charged, we often base our convictions on emotions instead of evidence.[2] By his frequent habit of ending his tweets with "SAD!", Donald Trump offers a practical illustration of this phenomenon. The result of politically motivated reasoning is a polarization and negation of the facts. What we believe about various issues becomes an effect of our political thinking rather than any well-founded knowledge or objective facts. It's the reason why political debates are so boring to watch nowadays – the opponents are mainly occupied with expressing what they *believe* and *think* and *feel,* often without any connection to facts.

Confirmation bias and politically motivated reasoning create excellent conditions for those who wish to disseminate fake news. By creating headlines that appear to confirm existing convictions, the creators of fake news lead us to click on links to learn more in the hope of having these convictions confirmed. One should keep in mind that there is money to be made in the advertising associated with the stories so that the more titillating and inflammatory the headline, the more money gets made by those fake news creators. This is a point worth making as there are some who don't care about the ideology and are only in it for the money.

One of the most notorious examples of fake news during the 2016 US presidential campaign was the Pope's supposed support for Donald Trump. Over one million people liked and shared this false article. (The Pope does not endorse political candidates.)

If we compare the 20 most popular news articles about the US election on Facebook in the four months preceding election day November 2016 with the 20 most popular "fake news" articles during the same period, we get an idea of just how strong an impulse confirmation bias is. The total number of reactions (likes, comments) to the fake news amounted to 8.7 million, compared to 7.3 million for the verified news![3]

The underlying purpose of social media, and all other digital services that offer personalization, is to persuade users to use the service in question as much as possible. The problem is that users have neither insight into, nor the ability to influence, the weight that algorithms attach to various types of personal information and behavior. There is no "off" button for algorithms if I would have preferred to view my friends' posts in the chronological order that is not possible today.

Over recent years, algorithms have been developed in an attempt to include things that I had no idea that I liked. This is done by comparing my individual profile with other profiles that are in some way similar to mine, and using information about what these other users like in order to suggest the same things to me. Put simply, the algorithm creates a stereotype that can be used to make assumptions about what I ought to like, and makes recommendations or suggestions accordingly. This is presumably why I never see articles about yoga in my feed, despite my interest in the subject. I am, after all, a man, and the stereotypical yoga practitioner is a woman. This is also a sign that an algorithm is never completely neutral. The biases and values of those who create algorithms affect the code. Normally we are oblivious to this, simply because the programmers themselves give no thought to it and we have no insight into the biases it introduces on our behalf.

Thus, there are many interacting factors that make it difficult to create an accurate worldview. Add to this the fact that the media landscape is considerably more fragmented than a few decades ago. It is easy to understand those who blame digital media, in general, for this development and who point out that social media contributes to a polarization of public discourse. Their proposed solution is to demand accountability on the part of these social networks and new platforms for their users' worldviews. By altering digital and social media algorithms to suggest news articles that challenge the user's worldview, they should be able to prevent the formation of filter bubbles. I have several reservations about such a proposal.

First, the proposal is based on the assumption that our worldview is *solely* formed by our social media feeds – as if we had never thumbed through a newspaper, never seen television news, never picked something up from the radio, or listened to our friends express their opinions on current affairs. Digital media alone cannot be blamed for the creation of filter bubbles. If you choose to read only a certain type of newspaper – perhaps with a more conservative bent – you also risk becoming trapped in a filter bubble.

Second, social networks and platforms are not democratic institutions. On joining, we accept terms and conditions that clearly stipulate that we can neither exercise influence over how the service is designed nor demand accountability for any undesirable effects that we may experience as a regular user.

Third, I am opposed to the idea that someone, or an algorithm, would diagnose my feed in order to ascertain whether my worldview is balanced and, thereafter, "medicate" me until such time as balance is restored to my news consumption. I understand that the intention is good, but the solution remains absurd.

The fourth reservation is simply to state the obvious; all

attempts to correct someone's self-image against their express wishes is in opposition to all liberal ideas about the individual's right to self-determination. ("My delusions may lack credence, but they are still mine.") Over the course of several decades, in many countries, the state's responsibility for – and, therefore, its ability to decide on behalf of – its citizens has decreased in favor of increased opportunities for citizens to take their own responsibility and make their own decisions. The idea that a corporation should take responsibility for ensuring that their users are generally educated, much in the way that the European welfare states sought to do for citizens in the mid-1950s, is as outdated as it is absurd.

A fifth reservation takes the form of a reminder about our ability to, consciously or unconsciously, create our own filter bubbles by searching for information that affirms our own worldview – our confirmation bias. Even if algorithms were to provide us with a balanced diet of news, we would still give greater weight to any news that confirms our understanding than to that which challenges it. (And we would be annoyed that irrelevant or uninteresting news is cluttering our news feeds.)

Nevertheless, I think I understand why this proposal arose. When we view filter bubbles as a technical challenge, we automatically search for a technical solution on which to pin our hopes. However, the problem is a more complex one than we can hope to solve by simply altering some algorithms. The problem is intrinsically linked to our inability to take responsibility for our own news diet, our ignorance of our inherent confirmation bias, and of the resulting confining filter bubble. If we are to solve the problem, we need general education on where the responsibility lies for the existence of filter bubbles – and that is with each and every one of us. Not with social media or the platforms, and it most certainly is not with the state but with you and me and everyone trying to obtain a balanced view of the world. The solution is to educate people about this responsibility, to help them take control of their information gathering, and perform basic source criticism. The realization that one exists within a big bubble of some kind is a first important step.

Deceptive filter bubbles

It seems to me both Donald Trump's and Hilary Clinton's campaign organizers were clearly unaware of the extent to which filter bubbles were polarizing the presidential election. Instead of an election campaign where all citizens were able to listen to or read the candidates' arguments on important social issues, it would be fairer to describe the Trump and Clinton campaigns as entirely separate parallel competitions aimed at getting the largest possible percentage of their own constituency into the polling station to vote. Rather than discussing policies or giving more thought to which arguments seemed attractive to their rival's supporters at campaign rallies, both sides resorted to describing their adversary in emotional terms as mentally unstable, or other unflattering terms.

One must remember that everyone who votes in an election does so because their choice seems somehow logical. To dismiss one's adversary in emotional terms as morally corrupt, and their supporters as ideologically extreme, poorly educated numbskulls, or as a self-righteous elite, is to subconsciously filter out facts that challenge our beliefs and restrict the opportunity to understand their world. This is an example of the politically motivated reasoning we spoke of earlier. Emotions affect our ability to make an objective judgement.

I once considered myself to be reasonably well-informed about US domestic politics. Since working as a volunteer on Barack Obama's first presidential campaign in 2008, I have followed US politics from a distance, with interest and admittedly through a liberal filter. This confirmation bias left me unable to understand how anyone could consider voting for Donald Trump. Fascinated by my own inability to grasp the idea, I manipulated Twitter's algorithm into recommending likeminded accounts so that I could create two separate bubbles fed by Republican and Democrat Twitter users, respectively. This allowed me to begin studying the bubbles from within, hearing the arguments as if I were an entirely normal Trump or Clinton supporter. In character, the bubbles were extremely similar to one another. Each had its influential voices, its fair share of fake news, its rowdy supporters, and loyal media outlets routinely ridiculing the other candidate. In both bubbles, astonishment was rife as to how the hell any reasonable person could even consider voting for the other bubble's dimwit candidate. Both bubbles seemed to scent victory. And yet, both sides expressed great surprise when the election results were in.

No one expected Donald Trump to win. Someone so politically inexperienced, with such a tarnished reputation as a New York real estate billionaire, should not have been able to win a primary, should not have been able to become a presidential candidate, and should not have been able to be elected president. If you were to compare him to previous candidates and the scrutiny they were subjected to, and the conduct that was expected before they could win the trust of the people and their vote, the result was unprecedented.

Filter bubbles are insufficient as an explanation for why Donald Trump won the presidential election. Then again, filter bubbles explain why so many people guessed wrong despite the signals that a Clinton victory was far from secure. When we see only what confirms our own worldview, it is inevitable that we will misinterpret signs to the contrary. Faced with the facts and with the demand to explain how they came about, it is perhaps unworthy of a political expert to point the finger of blame elsewhere, even if this is human. If you believe in your own objectivity, confirmation bias itself will ensure that the idea of being influenced by confirmation bias is dismissed before you even have time to consider the possibility.

After the unexpected Yes vote on Brexit in June 2016, many pundits laid the blame for the prognosticative fiasco squarely at the feet of pollsters. After the unexpected result in the US presidential election, criticism was primarily aimed at deceptive algorithms and the filter bubbles they create. Why had Facebook failed to enlighten its users of this possibility? Why did no alarms sound indicating that the message in the feed mirrored the monotonous reverberation of an echo chamber with false information swirling in the mix?

Audible echo chambers

Day-to-day behavior – such as how we use media, obtain news, or consume music – takes time to change. It is difficult to change behavior overnight. However, if change takes place in increments, we will perceive it as a simplification or as something people we know are already doing, and we will adapt ourselves surprisingly quickly and without giving it much thought. In order to show how much our media habits can change in only a few decades, we need only look at how the music industry has changed over the same period. The algorithms that control Spotify, Apple Music, and other streaming services offer us suggestions for new artists and new songs based on what we already like. Initially this seems great as the algorithms make our search for new music so much easier. However, as the artists suggested never deviate from a given genre, the feeling sneaks up on us that we have been consigned to an echo chamber. One day, not so long ago, it dawned on me that all of the artists suggested to me by Spotify were singer-songwriters. All that remained were slow, sonorous voices accompanied by guitar or piano. Norah Jones, James Blunt, Joni Mitchel, Ellie Goulding, Tracy Chapman. The problem is, that's not what I like. Not only, anyway. My musical taste is considerably more varied than that, but, for some reason, algorithms appear to have given more weight to these particular artists, something that first irritated me and then made me angry. Why weren't the algorithms fulfilling their function? And if that was the case, why couldn't I reset the algorithms or ask them to re-index the information in my listening history to correctly reflect my tastes?

If you compare the music feed with the news feed, there is no real difference; they both work in the same way and according to the same logic. The major difference is, of course, that you can hear when your music feed has become an echo chamber, quite literally. At certain points in this book, we will, therefore, take a diversion via music. By understanding how certain artists broke through and how the public reacted to the death of an artist, we can compare media habits at various points in time – how news is communicated and how it is received.

Donald Trump's relationship with music is largely unknown. However, in an interview with the BBC he did admit that he liked to listen to Frank Sinatra, Tony Bennet, Elton John, and Eminem. "If you love a certain kind of music, don't let other people's tastes influence your own," said Trump in his book *Think Like a Billionaire* (2004). "Whatever's the best for you is the best. Never forget that." This advice to create an echo chamber filled with music you already like is reminiscent of his desire to only receive positive news in his file of press clippings.

The most dangerous filter bubble of all is the belief that you have a handle on the situation. Of course, both algorithms and confirmation bias contribute to reinforcing this belief, but it also demands a degree of narcissism to believe that you already have an accurate picture of reality. An unwillingness to accept new information or influences from new sources is a worrying sign, implying as it does that you already have the necessary knowledge. Indeed, doubting your own understanding of the world is a sign of a sound mind.

PART 1.

A digital reality.

On Saturday February 11, 2012, just before 5 am local time, many television stations interrupted their regular broadcasts to announce the death of Whitney Houston. For the remainder of the day, CNN, MSNBC, Fox News, and others alternated images of the facade of the Beverly Hills Hotel – where Houston's body was discovered in Suite 434 – with interviews with those who had worked with, known, or lived near her. Across all forms of media, colleagues praised the deceased star. Mariah Carey and Quincy Jones were both of the opinion that she was the greatest singer of all time. Dolly Parton expressed her eternal gratitude that Houston had chosen to interpret her song *I Will Always Love You*, adding "Whitney, I will always love you." Aretha Franklin seemed most shocked of all. She explained that on first seeing news of Houston's death on television, she refused to believe it.[4]

Even though not many years have passed since Ms. Houston's death, our media habits have changed considerably. At the time of Ms. Houston's death in 2012, local TV stations were the primary source of information on breaking news for half of the US population, with her death being the main news item in bulletins for several days. Aretha Franklin then, was not alone in obtaining most of her information from television. Of course, many also learned of Ms. Houston's death online. On the list of sources from which people obtained news at least three times a week, the Internet was in second place with 46%, having passed the morning newspapers (40%) for the first time in media usage statistics[5].

News consumption in many parts of the world was largely similar to US habits at this time. In a comparison of which news sources people relied on most, the French, Germans, British, Spanish, Australians, and Japanese displayed the same behavior; television was their most important source. Only in Italy had the Internet replaced television as people's primary source. However, with regard to news about celebrities such as Whitney Houston, the Internet was the dominant news source in all countries except for Germany and Spain, something that can be attributed to their long tradition of celebrity-gossip magazines in print.

Whitney Houston died in the middle of a transition from analogue to digital media usage. Aretha Franklin saw the news of Houston's death on television, but sent her condolences on Twitter. Many others, however, heard about Ms. Houston's death via Twitter. In many countries outside the US, the news was first disseminated via Twitter, before other social media and far in advance of traditional media. The time of day was a factor. When news of Ms. Houston's death became public, it was already after midnight in Europe, and most television stations were off the air. The majority of newspaper editorial offices had already sent their morning edition to the printers. In Asia, it was morning or afternoon, and the day's newspapers had already been read. So, Twitter and Facebook were first out with the news. During the first hour after the news was released, the news was tweeted and retweeted almost 2.5 million times. Over the following days, many of the subjects and hashtags trending on Twitter globally were in some way connected to the singer's death: R.I.P Whitney Houston, #DearWhitney, #IWillAlwaysLoveYou, *The Bodyguard*, Bobby Brown and *I Wanna Dance With Somebody*.[6]

Whitney Houston died on a Saturday. On Sunday, the global media was packed with tribute articles by tearful music journalists describing the star's voice in rapturous tones. They offered personal anecdotes about their relationship to Ms. Houston, explained which of her songs meant the most to them, meant the most to the world. Readers, listeners, and viewers were treated to montages from her career, articles summarizing her path through life with a documentary eye, highpoints from her musical accomplishments. Add this to the articles listing Ms. Houston's most beautiful outfits, bizarre scandals, and outstanding live performances and those dealing with celebrity tweets – where they were when they heard the news about the identity of the body in

Suite 434 of the Beverly Hills Hotel. One week later, when the superstar was buried, she was mourned simultaneously by people from Maine to Manilla, Bogota to Belgrade, Cape Town to Kyoto.

Technology as an enabler

The digitalization of society has made it easier to find others who share a common interest. The shared sorrow experienced by so many after Whitney Houston's death is an example of this. The intellectual distance to someone in Bogota is not necessarily any greater than to someone in Berlin if these people share a fascination for Houston's voice and its astounding combination of velvety depths and chiming, airy heights. Someone in Manhattan may have more in common with someone in Queensboro than with someone in Queens when dissecting the intricacies of Ms. Houston's vocal technique when performing *The Star-Spangled Banner* before the 1991 Super Bowl. And even those who have not grown up with Ms. Houston's music, irrespective of whether they come from Malmö or Manchester, may feel exactly the same sense of wonder on hearing the near 45-second a cappella opening to her version of *I Will Always Love You*. A love of her music unites her fans regardless of location.

Digitalization has made the world feel smaller, but that feeling was seeping into our collective consciousness long before the age of computers. The feeling everything is connected began with the establishment of trade routes long before anyone understood that our planet was a globe. The flags flying on the stern of merchant ships signaled that they came from foreign lands, and the cargos they carried were a sign that people were no longer limited to the goods produced in their own locations. The advent of railway lines and passenger liners reduced this intellectual distance further, making it possible to travel to other places relatively quickly. Postal services allowed messages to be passed on seemingly from different worlds, the telegraph left only a negligible delay, while the telephone allowed communication in real time. Radio, and a little later television, contributed to the sensation of being part of a greater congregation that could simultaneously engage in one and the same story.

Music was a part of this. When, in the 1950s, popular culture as we understand it today began to spread across the Western World, music played an important role in carrying the message. In the wake of this music, adolescents discovered jeans, hamburgers, chewing gum, Coca-Cola, new brands of cigarettes, and other symbols that, at the time, became exclusively associated with young people. Historically, such symbols had always been associated with class or profession. Now symbols had become a sign of when one was born, of generational affiliation; the baby boomers. Never before had quite as much hope and expectation been placed on a single generation. Their parents had fought to provide their children with the very best in so many areas that these youths had come to represent the hope of a wiser, more peaceful and rational human race, capable of creating an ideal society. They were ready to rise above their parents' conflicts, their petty concerns with power and territory, and shoulder the burden of becoming responsible global citizens, of building stronger democracies in which inequalities could be eradicated. Perhaps allowances had to be made for this generation's strange clothes, their rock and roll music, and their admiration for mop-topped, pelvis-gyrating artists. Perhaps, despite everything, this was a reflection of the fact that those born after World War II represented the beginning of a better world order. Perhaps you had to accept the somewhat disconcerting fact that teenagers seemed more inclined to identify with their peers in other countries than with older generations in their own.

Technology enabled pop-culture

As so often before in human history, it was new technology that gave rise to shifting perspectives. FM radio, introduced in the years following the World War II, led to significantly improved sound quality. In the mid-1950s, the transistor radio was launched – battery-driven and small enough to carry with you. This meant that young people could both afford their own apparatus and choose stations that played the music they liked. Previously, the choice of channel had rested with parents. Of course, prior to this, other music had been widely disseminated; a wealth of classical music and opera reached an international public with the advent of the first record players and in the golden age of radio in the 1930s and 1940s. Nevertheless, that music and those artists pale in comparison to the idolization surrounding the music and artists that achieved fame in the 1950s and 1960s. The technical development of radio facilitated the evolution of a new form of youth culture, but it was pop culture that fueled it.

Just as jeans, hamburgers, and chewing gum represented something more than their base function, musicians embodied the ideals for which youth culture stood. Their songs and behavior signaled something about the inter-relationship between individuals and the individual's relationship with society, about views of authority and the individual's ability to achieve change. A generation of post-war children was only too pleased to be formed by this new ideal, by ideas that seemed to be shared by their entire generation. In the West at least. The founding of the United Nations and the adoption of the Universal Declaration of Human Rights in the 1940s signaled not only that all people had the same rights and obligations but also that an entire world shared these basic values. Of course, in reality this was, and remains, far from true, but it was in this belief that this new generation was raised.

They grew up believing themselves to be the first of their kind. All teenagers rebel against their parents' values, but this generation also believed that history was on their side.

Everything that could be associated with previous generations, and their experiences and opinions, was perceived as old-fashioned and, therefore, irrelevant to a group that above all else embraced the new. The baby boomers inherited the essential desire of their parents to move on after a devastating war, while ignoring their parents other wish – to learn from what had happened.

The rearview mirrors on postwar cars and motorcycles were, symbolically enough, small. The focus was firmly on progress, striving onward, developing. The baby boomers took this as a sign and turned their back on everything their parents had taught them. Caring for and repairing things got replaced by wear and tear. Rather than accepting one's fate and one' place in society like previous generations, they started to rock and roll. Forgetting about everything they've heard about the importance of duty and diligence, all they wanted to do was twist and shout. And why not? The majority of countries in the Western World experienced strong postwar growth, with jobs for all.

Parallel to this intellectual and technological evolution, a linguistic shift also contributed to a seemingly shrinking world, in any case among young people. Every empire has had its dominant language; Greek, Latin, Spanish, French, English, German. However, no language had ever previously laid claim to be the indisputable global language. English was the language of the victors but what established it as the indisputable global language was that young people *wanted* to learn it. The simple reason for this was that the coolest artists sang in English. These words were more than just their definition in a dictionary; they were also loaded with values, the values of someone with their gaze set firmly beyond their own national borders. This is still true today. Since the 1960s, artists from English-speaking countries have dominated the list of those famous enough to arrange world tours. All artists with ambitions to break through abroad sing in English, however, deficient their lyrics may be grammatically.

Popular culture established the United States as the cultural superpower it still is today; a continent where new trends are born to then spread around the world. The simple fact of something's Americanness is, in certain contexts, sufficient as a guarantee of quality and desirability. The platforms that dominate how we communicate with one another today have been assisted by the perception of the US as a futuristic land, meaning that we accept these platforms with less criticism than if, for example, they had come from Russia or China. It is easy to forget that they were created based on American customs and values, which should not be confused with global values (to the extent that it is even meaningful to speak of such). Google, Facebook, and Apple made their global breakthrough and gained acceptance precisely as jeans, hamburgers, and chewing gum did before them. Young people wanted them because they symbolized the values associated with the culture of the United States.

Without American music, no interest in American jeans, hamburgers, and chewing gum. Without music and culture, less interest in the English language and less of a perception of the world as a shrinking place. The Internet reinforced the feeling that we are connected and made it easier than ever, if so desired, to find people who share our interests, our values, and our musical tastes. The advent of social media reinforced that feeling even further.

Perhaps it is upon the demise of a beloved musician that the world feels at its absolute smallest. We read posts about the life-changing meanings that others attribute to certain songs and realize that we feel the same or that our stories have something in common, irrespective of where we live. Perhaps we are struck by how alike we humans actually are, despite all of our differences.

Seek and ye shall find something you already like

I am not a fan of Whitney Houston. Of course, I saw *The Bodyguard*, but I never bought her records, never saw her in concert. To my ears, all of her big hits sound alike. The main ingredients – the big voice, a soupçon of strings, the lovelorn lyrics, a dash of sentimentality – are always the same. It's not my thing. But maybe I'm wrong.

After all, this book is about escaping your bubble, so I decide to give her another chance and listen to an entire album. Which one should I choose? I search for "Whitney Houston" on Amazon and receive the reply that the album *I Will Always Love You* is the most relevant to me. The thing is, I have been an Amazon customer since time immemorial. Yes, me and Amazon go way back, to a time when all they sold was books and their logo was a half-hearted attempt to imitate the Amazon itself, sending customers' thoughts to the mighty river of literature to be found at this new online bookseller. Nobody knows more than Amazon about the kinds of books I like. They know that I have procured almost every book in existence about the history of BMW and draw my attention to any new book on the same narrow theme. They remember that I loved Margaret MacMillan's *The War That Ended Peace: How Europe abandoned peace for the First World War,* Tony Judt's *Post War,* Neil MacGregor's *Germany – Memories of a Nation.* When I searched for a book on the history of Sicily, their first suggestion was, therefore, a book in the same style; John Julius Norwich's *Sicily: A Short History, from the Greeks to Cosa Nostra.* I bought it and loved it, of course.

Amazon not only knows what I read, it knows *how* I read as well. They know that every May, I rush to buy the latest book in Alexander McCall Smith's *No.1 Ladies' Detective Agency* series as soon as it comes out in paperback. They know I like to read e-books. When they launched their e-book reader, I was one of the first to buy one (I'm now on my fourth Kindle). This means that I never find myself in the dreadful predicament of being without a book when travelling. In all likelihood, Amazon knows full well that I cried several times when listening to John Randolph Jones' narration of the audiobook of Sara Gruen's *Water for Elephants*, so gripped was I to hear the story brought to life.

Since then, the narrator is an important factor in my choice of audiobook. Amazon has duly taken note, among other things suggesting Douglas Coupland's *Hey Nostradamus!*, partly narrated by Jones.

However, Amazon cannot possibly know anything about my musical taste, as I have never purchased any music through them. So, the grounds on which they recommended that I begin with *I Will Always Love* You are somewhat of a mystery. Can they draw conclusions about my musical taste based on my literary preferences? Or was the Amazon recommendation based on a comparison between my reading habits and those of other users and a qualified guess about what music I *should* like based on what they had purchased? For this is, of course, what Amazon did when they became the first to introduce automated recommendations on their site ("Customers who bought this item also bought...") at the end of the 1990s, thereby sowing the seeds for today's filter bubbles. The term was a simple device to encourage people to buy one more book.

Although, hang on... It occurs to me that I'm not even logged in to Amazon. How then can they suggest *I Will Always Love You*? On a whim, I sort Whitney's albums based on which one has sold the best and I have my answer. Faced with a lack of information about my preferences, Amazon's algorithm has simply suggested the album by that artist that sells best. In all likelihood, if everyone else likes something, so will I.

Algorithms as assistants

I learned to code in an afternoon. That was in the late 1990s, while I was working as a designer for an advertising agency in Malmö, Sweden. I was young, the Internet was new, and we had been hired to construct a website for a company that sold tea and wanted to show that they were keeping up with technological developments. I asked my friend Niklas to teach me the basics of HTML in a couple of hours, so that I could pass myself off as the Internet expert I had painted myself as a couple of days previously. Niklas proved to be a good teacher, and I proved to be a receptive pupil. The simple logic appealed to me. All programs consist of code, many lines of commands that tell the program what to do and how to behave in various circumstances. Every line represents a task, designed as instructions and equations whose validity is dependent of a variety of conditions. A line of code on a website can tell the browser that it should have a white background, that the body text should be black, right aligned, located 65 pixels from the left-hand edge of the screen, and set in the font Georgia in a size of 18 pixels. Another line instructs the program to center an image on a logo at a size of 250 x 70 pixels and that the image should be downloaded from a given server. A third row instructs the program to show information, such as the best-selling book on an online bookshop (as Amazon did). A fourth row is even more sophisticated. It instructs the browser to investigate whether a visitor has visited the site before and, if so, to use the information to make a request to a database to obtain details of the types of articles the visitor has previously read, so that the browser can display more articles of a similar nature.

It is possible to code in many different languages, but the logic is always the same. The program reads the lines in a predetermined order and carries out the tasks; irrespective of whether the program contains instructions on a website's graphic design, how a robot should move in a factory to collect chassis components and place them in a predetermined location, or if it is to perform advanced calculations to analyze an X-ray for signs of early-stage breast cancer. All code follows a built-in logic.

When I learned to code at the end of the twentieth century, the world was still largely analogue. Today, it is mostly digital and controlled by code. Previously, when riding the subway, I would need to stamp my ticket. Today, automatic ticket barriers are programmed to read the identification number on my plastic travel card as I hold it over the reader, and then confirm with a central database that I have sufficient funds on my card to gain admission. If the answer is yes, the barrier opens. If the answer is no, a red lamp is lit. This procedure follows a preprogrammed logic and takes only a millisecond. Evolution has been rapid and has occurred in multiple areas of society. The reason is simple. A great many processes have been improved, streamlined and made much faster by digitalization compared to if they had remained analogue. Our world has been digitalized to such an extent that it is no longer meaningful to make a distinction between the digital and analogue worlds. Because everything digital is also programmed, it is important that as many people as possible learn to understand how code works, if only in theory.

My coding skills have proved to be surprisingly useful. Over 20 years, I have learned enough to be able to make simple adjustments to the code for a website if I want to make minor improvements. My insight into the fundamental structure of all code means that I understand that if a program, app, or machine is functioning poorly, it is not because of the code in itself but rather how the code is formulated. I am never angry with a machine because "it" is not behaving as I want. I understand that this behavior is the result of how someone has programmed it.

It has been important to me to ensure that my children have the opportunity to understand the basic principles controlling how all code works, just as I want them to gain a basic understanding of the logic behind mathematics. Today, useful tools are available that allow coding without the need to write lines of code as I did. One of the most famous is the freeware tool Scratch, developed at MIT Media Lab, which allows you to create and arrange colored blocks that represent various types of tasks in order to see how their order and different settings affect the final outcome. When my children first tried the tool, it took only a couple of hours before they were able to create a simple game and experience the joy of deciding how something should be controlled. That is a feeling I wish everyone could experience.

An algorithm is in this context a piece of code used to control how different things are to be displayed. In the early years of computing, the term "algorithm" was seldom used. However, as computer science departments began to appear at universities during the 1960s, programmers wanted to show that they were more than just technicians. They, therefore, began to describe their code as algorithmic, as this linked them to one of history's greatest mathematicians, the Persian scholar Muhammad ibn Musa al-Khwarizmi or, as he was known in Latin, Algoritmi.

By calculating a number of predetermined factors, an algorithm achieves a result that controls which information is to be displayed in a given context. Amazon hopes that I will buy a certain book or album that matches the information about my own or other users' behavior stored in their database. When I click on a page in order to look at Whitney Houston's albums, in a fraction of a second the algorithm will probably perform the following tasks:

1. Identify which album the user is interested in learning more about.
2. Send a request to the database asking it to compile a list of titles bought by other customers at the same time as the album in question.
3. Show the most popular album with the text "Customers who bought this item also bought...".

Jeff Bezos knew nothing about how a bookshop worked when he started Amazon in 1994. He wasn't even a bibliophile. However, he was interested in making money and understood that the publishing industry was ripe for change. Book dealers have always had two possible competitive edges; range and physical location. When Amazon began selling books online, they were able to offer customers an infinitely greater range of books and did away with location as a competitive advantage. In so doing, they reduced everything to price. Amazon priced their books lower than anyone else to attract as many customers as possible. In order to compensate for reduced margins, they needed to entice more customers to buy one more book, something that automated recommendations contributed to.

Mr. Bezos' ignorance of the industry proved to be an advantage. Had he known anything about books, he might have insisted that recommended books be within the same genre as the purchase, which is how traditional bookshops reason when recommending titles. However, as he knew nothing about the product as such, Mr. Bezos considered it sensible to base recommendations on sales data instead, an approach that has characterized Amazon's attitude to the products they sell ever since. When Amazon introduced algorithm-generated suggestions, sales increased. Their secret could be described as not caring *what* they sell but rather *how* they sell it.

Rumors of Amazon's success soon spread, and many others copied their methods. One of the first to follow Amazon was Netflix, at the time renting physical films, although after a few years it became industry standard. The concept was almost inconceivably effective. Of all films rented from Netflix in 2008, 60% were recommended. This even surpassed Amazon's equivalent figure of 35%[7].

Over the past decade, Amazon has refined its recommendation algorithm to also include our previous purchases, items we have already placed in our cart, items we have reviewed, and other users' purchases and reviews.[8] This has made Amazon even better at recommending products that we will probably like, products that go with items we have already placed in our cart, and products that we will probably like and that are also popular with a given category of customer. This works: just over one third of all purchases from Amazon result from recommendations. Netflix has also honed and improved their algorithms. It is estimated that as much as 75% of everything we watch on the service is the result of recommendations created by their algorithms.[9]

Jeff Bezos' presumption that the publishing industry was ripe for change proved to be on the money. However, he could never have believed that Amazon would come to occupy the dominant position it enjoys in the book trade. In the United States, Amazon is responsible for eight out of ten e-book sales, nine out of ten online book sales, and 99% of audiobook sales[10]. Their low-price strategy goes a long way to explaining their success, and books have been the loss leader for Amazon's successful expansion into many non-book categories.

Algorithms as weapons

Sometimes it's downright spooky just how accurate some online adverts seem to be. However, what might be considered as a sixth sense on the part of advertisers is probably the result of an algorithm that inspects your browser history and draws conclusions based on that. Many websites use cookies – a cute name for a couple of lines of code deposited on the user's computer/tablet/smartphone. This allows them to target advertisements at the user in other contexts outside of their own site. The purpose of this is, of course, to lure the user to return and make a purchase, although many see it as an invasion of privacy. I have heard many people offer this as an example of filter bubbles and how they surround us with information we are presumed to like, and I understand how this may be perceived as such. However, there is a small yet crucial difference. Text or image-based advertisements aimed at tempting someone to visit a certain website – a method known as remarketing – are based on an actual behavior (you have visited a retailer online and looked at a pair of brown loafers) that an algorithm is programmed to react to by showing a given advertisement that is directly linked to the act (viewing loafers), with the sole purpose of achieving a sale. In other words, a very simple and obvious line can be drawn between cause (looking at shoes) and effect (being shown an ad for those shoes). The algorithms that contribute to creating filter bubbles on social media are considerably more sophisticated and take into account many more factors when assessing which of your friends' posts should be displayed. The purpose of social media's algorithms is not primarily that you should make a purchase but rather that you be engaged in order to use the service for a longer period of time.

The adverts that seem to follow us online are a modern weapon in the battle for our money, a way for the various stakeholders to remind us that we should purchase whatever it was we were looking at in their particular web shop. Before we move on, it is also worth taking a look at an example of how algorithms can be used by web shops as a weapon to pressure suppliers.

In January 2014, Hachette found itself in conflict with Amazon. The French publisher refused to allow Amazon to dump prices on their e-books, as these were an important part of Hachette's revenue. Without the need to print and distribute physical books, the publisher's margins were higher for e-books than for printed examples. For their part, Amazon considered the publisher's margins to be too high. They wanted to use e-books as a loss leader. What should have been a routine negotiation between supplier and retailer developed into a conflict of principles played out in public.

Amazon made full use of their dominant position to apply pressure to Hachette. Their method? They adjusted their algorithm. Books by authors published by Hachette were suddenly harder to find on Amazon, with some disappearing entirely, while books from other publishers appeared higher up in search results[11]. In some cases, only the audiobook appeared. In order to demonstrate Amazon's price leadership to customers, they generally offer discounts on new books and best-sellers (another task handled automatically by algorithm). However, suddenly this no longer applied to Hachette's books. Strangely enough, delivery times for Hachette books also seemed to be longer than for all other books, up to four weeks in some cases.[12] "We regret the inconvenience," declared Amazon in a written statement. They even went as far as to encourage customers to purchase the book from someone else than Amazon[13]. The changes to the algorithm resulted in plummeting sales of Hachette books from Amazon.

Even a physical bookseller can choose to act in a similar way in order to pressure a supplier. They can choose whether to display a new best-seller piled high and discounted just inside the door, where customers can hardly miss it, or place it on a bottom shelf at the rear of the store. What Amazon did can hardly be classed as censorship. Still, if a company is responsible for almost half of the book sales in a country, it is, nevertheless, hardly honorable to treat a supplier in this manner. Their behavior led to a great many protests from publishers, authors, and consumers. After eleven months, the parties eventually managed to reach an agreement. Neither of them wished to comment on its content[14]. This dispute demonstrated, with as much clarity as can be desired, just how important and powerful algorithms have become in influencing consumer behavior. Since then, their significance and impact has only increased.

Just like any other code, algorithms are ostensibly neutral, factual, logical. They are created to help users get a better experience, but, generally, they also attempt to manipulate the user into acting in a desired manner. In Amazon's case, the intent was just as clear as the method; the algorithm was altered to prevent customers from buying books from a specific supplier and the result was obvious. In most other cases, manipulation takes place in the shadows.

Artificial intelligence

How much do you know about your digital identity? By "digital identity" I mean not just the selected images that end up on Instagram or the structure of your CV on LinkedIn, but something greater. Our digital identity is created both by what we display and how we act, by the fragments of digital information we send to each other, the information we freely surrender to some organization, and the information we unwittingly, and often involuntarily, leave in our wake whenever we act online. Every time we text or email or check out a cat video, we contribute to this digital identity. All data can be logged, inspected, saved and used in future digital interactions. The question is, who owns all that data?

One standard position adopted by companies that collect data from their customers on a somewhat larger scale, is that they give their customers control over "some" of this information. In practice, this means that the company has control rather than the customer. The company considers the data as their own and view the issue of how they use the data as a business secret. Secrets are not fertile ground for trust, and, in recent years, discussions over the rights to one's own information have become more frequent and more voluble. (For some companies, the business of selling data has even become a critical asset and a business strategy.) The "right to be forgotten," i.e. that users should be able to request that a company deletes all information it holds about the user, is being enacted into law in several European countries. This, naturally, creates business opportunities for those companies that are willing to allow users a greater level of control over their data. Spanish Telecom operator Telefonica was one of the first companies to declare such an intention.[15] *All* data? No, absolutely not. A little bit more, but not all.

Social media are most associated with their algorithms. Facebook, Instagram, YouTube, Snap, WeChat, Twitter, LinkedIn, Weibo – they all analyze our opinions and provide us with more of the same. Posts from the friends we have the most contact with are prioritized over those from people we don't appear to like as much.

And what about search engines? Yes, even those. Both Bing and Google have algorithms that decide which results are the most relevant based on what previous users have clicked on, and they sort and filter accordingly. They also use information about the searcher (and other searchers) in order to make assumptions about what we will consider most relevant when the search results are presented. This explains the story circulating online that two people do not necessarily see the same results despite googling the same thing. Google's intentions are good – as well as commercially motivated – as the aim is to be able to present the most relevant results possible for the specific searcher, in the hope that they will use the same search engine next time. There is no doubt that Google has become more proficient at giving us the answers we're looking for; their dominant position is proof of this.

This driving force – to make visitors feel that what they see on a website is specifically relevant to them – is the reason almost all large stakeholders use algorithms today. Commercial retailers such as H&M, Zara, and Target. Non-commercial organizations such as the BBC and PBS. Prestigious newspapers such as *Süddeutche Zeitung* and *Le Monde*, as well as those with academic creditability such as the *Harvard Business Review*.

Researchers at Cambridge and Stanford universities have confirmed that it requires surprisingly little data on a user for an algorithm to be able to create a nuanced picture of their personality and demographic. A group led by scientist Vesselin Popov has demonstrated that it is sufficient to analyze which pages someone likes on Facebook to create an accurate psychometric profile of the same standard as a psychological profile generated based on personality tests containing several hundred questions. This includes assumptions on personality type, intelligence, life satisfaction, political opinion, religion, sexuality, profession, age, gender, and whether the person is in a relationship or not. Using information on as little as ten pages a person has liked, the algorithm is able to provide a more accurate description of a person's personality than the average person's colleagues. If the algorithm is provided with information on 150 likes, it is more accurate than the person's family and with 300 likes, it is able to surpass the person's life partner. The conclusion, then, is that, in all probability, Facebook knows you better than your friends do.[16]

For those that are interested in understanding more about how digital identities can be used to analyze personal characteristics, Mr. Popov and his team created a tool, *applymagicsauce.com*, so that you can see your psychometric profile based on data supplied to Facebook and Twitter. This is a useful exercise in a secure setting (results are not saved) to raise awareness of just how many conclusions an algorithm can draw based on the data that social networks store about you. A reasonable ambition would be to attempt to understand your own digital identity as well as these corporations do. I suggest you give the tool a try.

According to Mr. Popov, most people are willing to accept customized ads as long as they also understand which data has influenced said customization. However, that is not currently the situation. When you use your Facebook profile to log in somewhere, the company may, depending on how the login is programmed, collect information about which sites you like and use that information to create the psychometric profile of you that can help them to understand what types of argument will appeal to you. According to *applymagicsauce.com*, my weakness for musician John Mayer signals that I am somewhat less intelligent. On the other hand, it suggests that I have higher than average life satisfaction. John Mayer also makes me appear a little gayer. Then again, I like Starbucks, which apparently makes me appear a little straighter.

A company doesn't even need access to your Facebook profile to create a psychometric profile of you. They can also purchase data on the open market from a data broker. Everything seems to find a buyer, even sensitive information such as credit reports and credit card purchase history. Donald Trump's presidential campaign partly used purchased data and psychometry to decide which voter groups should be exposed to which types of message. This also included opponents' data in order to reach them with ads convincing them not to vote at all. The purpose was to get the people you need to vote to understand the importance of getting themselves to the polling station by telling them the margins are small and, at the same time, making your opponents fans believe that the victory was so certain there really is no need for them to vote.

Algorithms that learn from us

Every new advance made since the introduction of the computer in the 1980s has required people to learn new techniques. We learned keyboard shortcuts and other tricks to get programs to do our bidding, but this remained so sufficiently convoluted that we were willing to change our software, our hardware, our peripherals as soon as another product was launched that seemed easier to understand and use.

Take our method of consuming music as an example. There were many other ways to find music online when Apple launched iTunes in 2001, but none of them made it as easy to download and pay for music. The same goes for the iPod. The market was awash with MP3 players, but none of them provided such a simple system for transferring music from a computer, and none were as easy to use. This also applies to Spotify. The service took off because, as a method of consuming music, it was quite simply vastly superior. At a fixed monthly cost, you can obtain access to almost all music ever recorded. Since I live in Stockholm, I received an early invitation to join from someone who knew someone who worked at Spotify. I installed the program, satisfied myself that the service indisputably contained a vast amount of music that I liked, and I haven't used an iPod or iTunes since.

The code that controls how digital devices function indirectly influences how we interact with them in order to make them do what we want. Until now, we humans have been required to learn how to use devices correctly. Through the use of algorithms that can draw conclusions and make assumptions, devices are becoming ever smarter. Instead of learning to understand them, they are beginning to learn to anticipate and even understand us. This is known as artificial intelligence or AI, and, in its simplest form, it means allowing a machine to imitate human behavior. The difference between a machine controlled by code and a machine programmed to have a certain level of AI is that the first will repeat exactly the same behavior under given conditions, while the latter is able to draw conclusions and vary its behavior accordingly. To this end, it uses algorithms and applies predetermined logic to evaluate various types of data.

However, a machine (or program) can also learn things independently. This is called "machine learning" and means that the machine is permitted to study behavior and, in so doing, learn to replicate it without the need for any human supervision. This works by allowing algorithms to train by analyzing large amounts of data and drawing conclusions while, at the same time, receiving information on the extent to which these conclusions are right or wrong. Feedback is used to adjust how different types of data are to be evaluated. An algorithm designed to learn how to identify cancer cells on an X-ray will make many mistakes at first, but, given the opportunity to train on millions of X-rays of documented cancer cells, it will eventually become so proficient that it will be able to identify malignant cells with greater accuracy than an experienced doctor.

An even more advanced method for allowing machines to develop artificial intelligence is through "deep learning."

This is done by providing the machine with large amounts of data that can be used to draw conclusions about other data the machine also has access to. As computers are able to make millions of calculations in a short period of time, correlations can be identified that would take humans a far greater amount of time to discover. Such as that the probability that a person is gay increases if he or she likes John Mayer on Facebook but decreases if he or she likes Starbucks.

Despite the rapid pace of development, today's AIs are still not particularly smart in comparison to any human. Most AIs we come into contact with are narrow, meaning that they can carry out one task well but lack the ability to solve complex problems. The all-knowing AI so often portrayed in Science Fiction is at the other end of the spectrum, what is normally referred to as strong or general AI. These are characterized by an ability to think broadly and from a systems perspective, something we humans are good at. The difference between these extremes can, therefore, be described as the difference between vertical and lateral thinking.

All of the devices, programs, and digital services we use today are programmed and use algorithms to draw conclusions from the data we provide. This contributes to an improved (and filtered) user experience. However, sometimes it results in a much worse experience.

Hasty conclusions

The digital is no longer something confined to a certain device, a computer, tablet or a phone. It has become something that continuously surrounds us, with our phones acting as universal remote controls. Artificial intelligence means that, in the future, we will no longer need to reach for our phones to search for the various kinds of information we require on a daily basis but can instead ask our phones for help to complete our everyday tasks. In order to navigate this digital day-to-day existence in the manner that best suits us, we will need to rely on our digital servants – assistants and bots.

Assistants need to be smart in the broader sense, conversational characters that can respond when addressed, both vocally and in writing, to ease our daily burden. An assistant can review my inbox to identify tasks I have promised to undertake but have yet to perform and, then, warn me. Or suggest a suitable response to an email based on an analysis of the sender's preferred language usage.

The most common assistants are named Google, Siri, Alexa, and Cortana (the feminist in me naturally wonders why three of these have been given female names) and come from Google, Apple, Amazon, and Microsoft. They sometimes give the impression of being new to the job, but, as they develop, they quickly learn new tricks and skills. Siri, for example, can guess what you will want to search for online next, based on your previous requests for help or what you have just read. Assistants can also take care of those tasks that unnecessarily take up so much time at meetings. One participant's Cortana can inform the other participants' assistants: "This is Kiara and these are his preferences for this particular meeting room, and this is what he wants displayed on the projector while he gives his presentation[17]".

If an assistant's task is to get to know our needs and make suggestions accordingly, the primary task of bots is to perform the work. They are small programs of limited intelligence, created to automate or simplify tasks you once performed yourself, such as reserve a table at a restaurant or pay an invoice or, in Kiara's case, make sure that the projector has the images for his presentation. Instead of trawling eBay for a brown leather handbag, simply tell a bot your requirements, and it will send suggestions direct to your messaging app.

My personal favorite, Mica, the Hipster Cat Bot, is a bit stupid yet pretty cute bot on Messenger that helps me find hip bars and restaurants. All I need to do is send an emoji with the type of food or drink I'm in the mood for, and Mica will make a suggestion based on my current location. Mica also accepts very simple text messages asking for advice on other towns and cities. Should Mica fail to find anything, or understand what you mean (a relatively frequent occurrence), it will send you a cute cat picture by way of response.

As we come to rely more and more on digital assistants to facilitate our daily lives, the need to be able to trust them under all circumstances also increases. When Siri recommends the optimal route to somewhere, there must be no suspicion that Dunkin' Donuts has paid to ensure that we pass as many of their establishments as possible. When we ask Cortana for advice on finding a good laptop, we should not feel that she is favoring a Microsoft product. And when we ask Alexa, we must be able to count on her impartiality. Otherwise, if Hachette finds itself in dispute with Amazon again – what is to stop Alexa from denying the very existence of their books?

We are only at the beginning of the development of artificial intelligence, and, while it is impossible to say what advances the next five years will bring, we can say that, in all probability, AI will be able to do things that seem impossible to us today. At the same time, the demands that we can, should, and have the right to make of companies that use algorithms also increase. Even if they refuse to reveal exactly how their algorithms work – just as Coca-Cola refuses to reveal its original recipe – it is not beyond the realms of possibility that even tech companies will be forced to declare the content of their products. What data is their algorithms using and what data is given most importance? And what rights do you have to delete, correct or modify the data?

Confirmation bias

Just like economics, computer science is founded on a preconceived view of the world and human nature. These views are generally a result of how the world looks to programmers. But what if a woman asks Siri for a suggestion as to where she can buy skin tone tights? Will Siri then take into account the skin color of the person asking the question or automatically suggest light beige tights, so long the norm in the West? Is the Spanish-language version of Cortana more Catholic than the English-language version? Does Alexa know which hotels accept gay couples as guests and which don't? The answer depends on how the assistant is programmed, which, in turn, depends on the thought processes of the programmer.

Therefore, digital assistants are never better than their code. If the programmer doesn't take into consideration that the term "skin color" will have a different meaning for different people, then neither will the assistant. If the person programming an assistant is unaware of their own preconceived notions, so will the assistant be unaware.

How the brain actually functions is still somewhat of a mystery. In fact, not even researchers are entirely sure. The brain's method for drawing conclusions based on impressions is not outwardly dissimilar to how an algorithm draws conclusions, but we are not entirely sure as to how this happens. The brain consumes more energy than any other bodily organ. Anyone who has had many new experiences during a single day knows how tiring, both mentally and physically, it can be for the brain to process all of these impressions. In order to minimize energy consumption, your brain is, therefore, programmed to search your memory for impressions similar to the new sensations to which it is being exposed. If suitable memories are accessed, your brain will use the previous analysis in the current situation. In order to save energy, your brain is coded to take a shortcut.

This is the neurological explanation for prejudices. The first time you see a man on stage telling you that he's Jewish, without knowing how to interpret the information, your brain will make a note. If the Jewish man up on stage tells jokes and you laugh at them, your brain will make an assessment that *Jewish + Man + Stage = Funny*. The next time you see a Jewish man on stage, your brain will use the same analysis, the same assessment. If he also proves to be funny, your brain will interpret this as positive feedback and, by indulging in a little machine learning, decide that the previous assessment was indeed correct, improving the ranking of this conclusion in the list of possible conclusions to be drawn when encountering a Jewish man on stage. (If the second Jewish man isn't funny, the assessment will be weakened, and your brain will return to doubting how to interpret the information.) If you then encounter a third Jewish man who is equally funny but is not on stage, your brain will apply deep learning and ascribe the stage somewhat reduced importance in the assessment of what signals that the presence of a Jewish man means things will be funny. I'm sure you understand where this line of reasoning leads. Prejudices are quite literally judgements we make of people we have never met based on our experiences of similar people.

This characteristic was of practical use a few thousand years ago when our lives could balance on the ability to quickly decide if someone was friend, or a potential enemy with whom a certain level of suspicion was a wise strategy. Even if the circumstances under which we live have changed radically since then, our brains are still coded in the same way today. In order to compensate for a prejudice, you must first be aware of its existence. This is not easy. Our brains are coded to search for confirmation of those things we already consider to be true. Perhaps this is also a way to conserve energy? In any case, this is the phenomenon known as "confirmation bias" because our desire to have what we already know confirmed makes us biased and unable to make a sober judgement of an unfamiliar situation, historic event, or new information that comes into our possession. Since the 1960s, many experiments have been carried out on confirmation bias, and the phenomenon is well-founded.[18] When attempting to check if a news item is true, we, therefore, prefer to look to sources that we, whether consciously or subconsciously, believe will confirm our own beliefs, and we discard those sources that seem to us uninteresting or irrelevant. A pessimist may, therefore, be understood as someone with a negative confirmation bias who constantly sees the world in the worst possible light. Confirmation bias reinforces a preconceived notion.

Just like algorithms, the human brain is never neutral, but, rather, it is colored by its previous conclusions, the prejudices it has constructed over time, and the confirmation bias that cements these. Think of this as the IKEA effect – the tendency to set greater store by something simply because you assembled it yourself. The same can be said about your self-assembled theories.

Algorithmic discrimination

Since there is a risk that a programmers' prejudices will influence how an algorithm is coded, the result of an algorithm's calculations may have serious consequences. Algorithms control more than just our news feed – they are everywhere. Algorithms calculate your credit score when you need a loan, measure how many calories you burn when you jog, control the air conditioning in your living room so it's cool when you arrive home, predict the demand for taxis in your neighborhood, and calculate the distance to other vehicles so that cars can drive themselves.

The built-in logic in all code means that algorithms can also be understood as mathematical equations designed to weigh up a number of factors and present a result. What these factors are depends on whose algorithm you are dealing with. In order to decide what content should be shown to you specifically, some of the following factors will generally be weighed up; the types of posts you read previously, the time of day, the phone you use, your age, your location, the sites you visited previously.

Other services use other types of data to allow algorithms to calculate how best to satisfy their customers' needs and, at the same time, maximize the company's profits. Skype uses algorithms that translate several languages in real time, making it easier for people to speak to one another. Supermarkets use algorithms to analyze the types of food you normally buy, so that special offers can be tailored to each customer. H&M uses algorithms to analyze sales statistics (to quickly see which products are and are not selling) and product feeds (to predict which product will need to be dispatched to which stores). Another example is Uber, which has an algorithm to calculate where in a city most vehicles will be required at any given point in time and another to control dynamic pricing (as demand rises, so do prices). The effect of Uber's calculations could mean that the chance of finding an Uber vehicle is reduced in poor areas in comparison to rich areas of the same city. This may seem cynical, but it is the logical and mathematical result of the efforts of two algorithms to optimize customer satisfaction and company profits.

This may lead to some people being excluded from certain contexts – something that can be a form of discrimination. Let us say that we have a bank that uses an algorithm that attempts to predict who will be a good customer and who will not. If consideration is given to the average income in different districts, those living in low-income districts may find it harder to get loans as the algorithm making the credit assessment tars everyone in that neighborhood with the same brush. Of course, the same phenomenon may also mean that a home insurance premium varies from district to district, disadvantaging those with higher incomes because they can afford to pay more.

Algorithmic discrimination is a new yet certainly growing problem. I've heard stories about a voice recognition software that struggled to understand women since it was mainly trained on male voices[19], the crime prediction algorithm that targeted black neighborhoods since it reinforced bad police habits[20], and the online ad platform which was more likely to show men highly paid executive jobs[21].

Algorithms are our new laws, affecting our everyday lives, but leaving us with no democratic opportunity to influence them. Very few companies currently reveal what motivates their algorithms in their surveillance of us. In all likelihood, this will change over the next few years. It is conceivable that, in the same way that the food industry must disclose the ingredients in their ketchup, retailers will be forced to disclose how they use the data generated when we buy the ketchup in their store.

The demand to divulge the factors that algorithms take into account is most often directed towards Google, Facebook, and Microsoft – the companies behind some of the Internet's most popular free services. However, can you really make any demands of a company of which you are not a customer? You may have used Google to search for information several times a day throughout the twenty-first century, and, yet, you will never have been required to pay for it. You may have used Hotmail for ten years without once needing to reach into your wallet. You may have used

Facebook for five years without giving them a single dollar, euro, or yen in exchange for the right to use the services they provide. What right, then, do you have to ask for something in return?

Another way to look at it is that you have, in fact, paid by giving them information about yourself, information that they use to sell advertising space. Online, we have become accustomed to the idea that the price of convenience is the sacrifice of a certain degree of privacy. Before the Internet, credit card companies and credit bureaus were alone in making such an offer. In exchange for a little personal information, and the opportunity to see all of your purchases, you could receive a card that relieved you of the burden of carrying cash. Life became a little more convenient.

One of the major factors in the internet's breakthrough was that all information appeared to be free of charge. This assumption is beginning to change, driven not the least by those media outlets that have begun to charge for unique content. Still, there remain many passionate advocates of universal freedom of information. This is an attitude that stands in stark contrast to how things work in the real world, where there is no such thing as a free lunch. In some way, sooner or later, that lunch needs to be paid for. The same logic applies online. When we use personal information as currency to pay corporations for ostensibly free services, those corporations must, sooner or later, find a way to monetize that information.

The price we pay for using free services is our unwitting

consent to be enclosed in a bubble in which the corporation controls what we see and what is withheld from us. Or if you will, to allow algorithms to discriminate against our obtaining an accurate image of the world.

The dangers of filter bubbles

The term "filter bubble" was coined in 2011 by journalist Eli Pariser who, in an attention-grabbing speech, described the dangers inherent in never having your views and preconceived notions challenged by other perspectives.[22] That an individual citizen may have a somewhat skewed worldview is something that society can manage, but what happens when the worldview of every citizen is skewed? A strong democracy is dependent on its citizens being able to see things from each other's perspectives, but it seems that we are increasingly moving towards a life enclosed in our own bubbles. For a public discourse to be meaningful, we must be able to begin from underlying facts. However, today we seem to live in parallel universes, where entirely separate opinions of what is true prevail and where tribalism is reinforced digitally.

After his talk, Mr. Pariser wrote a book on filter bubbles. Its disposition is reminiscent of every other book warning of technological threats, in which the author by turns cries out that the wolf is at the door, the end is nigh, and, then, implies that the technology is the result of a wolf conspiracy. However, according to Mr. Pariser, the solution is not to teach the people to defend themselves against wolves or uncover conspiracies, but rather to domesticate the wolves through legislation. I shall refrain from going any deeper into the case made by the book, suffice to say that Mr. Pariser came to his understanding of the size of this threat long before the use of algorithms became as frequent and sophisticated as it is today. Today, the wolf is here and living among us.

On December 4, 2016, a 28-year-old man walked into Comet Ping Pong, a pizzeria in Washington DC, and fired three shots from a rifle. His motive? He had read online that child sex slaves were being held in the restaurant and wanted to investigate if this was actually the case. The shots ricocheted around the walls of the restaurant, but no one was injured. What the man had read was a conspiracy theory that had blossomed during the 2016 presidential campaign. It began with the hacking of Hilary Clinton's campaign manager's email account and the publication of some of the emails on WikiLeaks. The theory was based on the otherwise boring content of the emails being in code, and the discussion of what food to order being in reality a list of pedophile preferences. In other words, these emails were supposed to link members of the Democratic Party to certain designated restaurants that held children as sex slaves. This was the core of the theory that came to be known as "Pizzagate" and that quickly grew into a wild thicket of "evidence" that the Democratic leadership was corrupt and considered itself above the law. A surprisingly large group apparently considered this theory to be credible, including the 28-year-old man in question, saying "the intel on this wasn't 100 %".[23] (The shooter was sentenced to four years in prison.[24])

However crazy the theory might appear, it was entirely in line with Donald Trump's description of the corrupt and "crooked Hillary". Pizzagate, therefore, says something about how confirmation bias can deform a person's perception of reality, even if it is an extreme example of the societal problems algorithms can cause in their attempts to give users more of what they already like. Like that time NASA had to officially deny that it was holding child slaves on Mars.[25] To have government agencies officially have to issue public statements speaks volumes about how much of a problem this has become.

When Eli Pariser gave his Ted Talk in 2011, he illustrated the contribution of search engines to the creation of filter bubbles and the reinforcement of erroneous worldviews. He asked two friends to google "Egypt" and then take a screenshot of their results. These search results looked very different. One person received information about the political turmoil plaguing the country at the time. The other person, strangely enough, saw nothing about this in their search results but was exposed solely to information about Egypt as a tourist destination. Did Google customize its answers based on who was conducting the search?

Google's algorithm takes into account a number of factors. If you search for factual information (say, Japan's area), you will receive a correct answer. However, if you search for the answer to something more complicated (say, why a historical figure did something) you will run into problems. Google will never reply: "It is difficult to give a definitive answer," but rather it will display a deceptively objective list of different results. One may forgive those who without reflection assume that the order of this list is decided by a comparison against known facts or what other people have found to be relevant. What Mr. Pariser had seemingly uncovered was deeply problematical; answers were tailored to the assumptions made by Google based on what the search engine knows about us. Two people searching for an answer to the question of who Anders Behring Breivik is may, therefore, receive different answers. Norwegian freedom fighter or deranged mass murderer? It's up to you to decide. Or rather, the search engine will decide based on what it already knows about you.

The helpful bubble can quickly become sinister. It is entirely possible that filtered feeds and customized search results reinforced the delusions that Anders Behring Breivik had developed about the ongoing ethnic cleansing of the Norwegian people, and the need to act to stop it. In the anti-Islamic milieu in which Mr. Behring Breivik moved, the idea of the impending downfall of and ongoing war against their own people was common currency. This anti-Islamic movement warned against the impending creation of an Arabic Europe – Eurabia – through a secret agreement between the West and the Arab world. Just like Pizzagate, conspiracy theories of this kind seem wholly implausible to outsiders. To those who believe in them, however, they are only too real. With every Google search query, they can find confirmation. Every time they open the Facebook app, they see posts from others as proof that the conspiracy exists. That an individual citizen may have a somewhat skewed worldview is something that society can manage – but what happens when everyone in a tribe shares it? This is the direction we're heading in.

How do you know if something is true?

I share Mr. Pariser's concern that we are moving towards a society in which everyone considers themselves to be at the center of an egocentric planetary system that seems to revolve around them. A society where we live next to one another instead of with one another in a shared community. A society where friends no longer gather around the campfire on weekends, but, instead, spend them alone in the glow of a screen. A society in which we transfer to our daily lives the virtual behavior of ignoring those with different opinions, instead of understanding that multiple perspectives can color a monochrome world.

The evolution of technology will no doubt surprise us as much over the next decade as it did the last. Social networks will become more socially sophisticated and machines more human. However, they will never offer a hug, never compensate for the fact that someone dear to you may be elsewhere instead of sitting next to you, never replace physical presence. Strong societies are not created from a collection of likeminded people; they are the product of interactions between people who might see things very differently but who collaborate nonetheless. It is not necessary to like one another in order to respect the right to exist. You may think that I'm wrong about something, but, as long as we can agree on certain basic facts, there remains something to discuss, to change, to improve. The most dangerous thing about filter bubbles is that they contribute to a society in which what can be considered facts differs from bubble to bubble.

Seen in this light "alternative facts" are a fraudulent attempt to pass off the insubstantial as solid matter. An "alternative fact," however, is still a lie, and a fact is still a fact. Statistical facts (for example, Japans' area or the size of the crowd that attended Donald Trump's inauguration) are easily corroborated.

Facts about current events present more difficulties. One approach is to do the job yourself. Find as many independent sources as possible or check the "facts" against a source certified by a credible expert, and then draw your own conclusions. But it might still not be enough.

Academics speak in terms of epistemology and ontology, the study of knowledge and of the nature of existence, respectively. You do need not to get overly bogged down in this, but it is valid to ask yourself the question: what do I consider to be facts? Because the specter of confirmation bias looms. If you want to discover the truth about something, begin by asking yourself "What is the truth?" and "Whose truth are we talking about?".

As a historian, I am bound to the source material. Conventionally, this material will be written, either by hand or in print. It is these remains that a person examines in order to try to understand a traumatic event that took place long ago. However, this material is not sufficient to describe the feelings of those who experienced the event, the fear they felt when faced with this trauma. Add to this the fact that much of this material is written from the perspective of those in power; civil servants, doctors, politicians. Occasionally you may find a letter from the victim of a trauma, testifying to persecution or abuse. Nevertheless, we see only a sliver of reality – of the truth that they experienced. Sometimes those who experienced the events are still alive, or at least their family or friends. These interviews, memories, and recollections contribute a few more pieces to the puzzle, and, sometimes, that is enough to create a clear enough picture of an event for us to understand it from different perspectives.

All historical depictions are also depictions of the present. History is often reinterpreted and exploited for political gain in the here and now. Rewriting history is not automatically a bad thing. There are advantages to living in a country in which the past is open to question, as the descriptions we have of many past events have lost contact with historical reality. The important thing in all historical debate is that some kind of recalibration takes place in which opposing "truths" about events eventually contribute to a more nuanced picture of history. Nevertheless, this new picture must be rooted in historical fact.

As a journalist, to some extent I contribute to contemporary history through my writing. As a member of the Swedish Union of Journalists, I have undertaken to abide by certain ethical guidelines, and, similarly, the media I work for comply with the publication regulations applicable to press, radio, and television. Our point of departure is that our task is to report the news accurately. Public trust demands that we accurately and impartially report on current events. This implies that we criticize the sources of our news, that we check our facts as carefully as circumstances allow, even if they have been published previously elsewhere. The task of ensuring that facts are correct on every occasion is far too important for us to trust that a colleague has carried out their job correctly.[26]

In an age when trust in the media is being eroded and when the media is being accused of publishing fake news, fact checking is even more important. Over recent years, there have been several cases where journalists have published stories based on facts later revealed to be skillful fabrications. There are good reasons for believing that these were planted solely to discredit the media organizations these journalists worked for. There are even organizations that have arisen to test publications to take the bait of fabrications such as the ironically named Project Veritas which purports to expose media bias and has tried to trick the Washington Post among others.[27]

So, how do you know if something is true? The answer is that you can never be one hundred percent certain but the probability increases when sources and facts are clearly reported.

What are tech companies responsible for, really?

But what good are facts against people whose convictions are set in stone, people driven by a desire to confirm their theory? Conspiracy theories are nothing new. Delusional crackpots have always been with us. What constitutes an objective view of the present is something people have disputed for thousands of years. Hasn't the answer always been very different depending on who you ask and how that person sees the world? How the world is experienced by a person has always been filtered through preconceived notions formed by childhood environment, class, religion, education, income and social circle.

Many others share Eli Pariser's concerns over the direction we are moving in. Many millions have seen his Ted Talk warning of the effects of filter bubbles.[28] He was among the first to demand accountability from corporations in creating a balanced worldview for their users. Mr. Pariser proposed that, by changing their algorithms, the companies behind the platforms should ensure that users are both exposed to articles that contradict their opinions and to more important news.[29] The wolves should be leashed and re-schooled to become useful tracking dogs. As I explained in the introduction, however well meaning, this proposal is naive on several levels. I dislike both the idea of a corporation deciding what news is socially beneficial and of freeing citizens from any responsibility for their own worldview.

Tech companies however, are not without responsibility for these developments. In comparison to bygone bubbles, our digital bubbles are both involuntary and more restrictive. Where once the cultivation of a delusion required a certain level of effort and perseverance, algorithms now simplify the process. If you only click on what you like, you will soon be relieved of seeing everything else. This is the paradox we live in. Thanks to digitalization, never before in human history has it been so easy for someone to obtain a broad perspective on the world. At the same time and thanks to the same digitalization, it has never been easier to narrow our viewpoint – almost entirely without effort. Corporations have driven developments in this direction out of a desire to earn greater advertising revenues. So they certainly have a responsibility.

We define our lives through digital platforms; describe our careers on LinkedIn, share things we read on Twitter, our daily lives on Instagram, the moment on Snapchat. We place our lives in their hands, quite literally, when what we upload is stored on their servers.

These platforms, however, are never neutral – they are

not railroad lines. Nevertheless, it is often as railroad lines that they are described. As means of communication that make it easier for us to come into contact with others, neither more nor less. Nevertheless, women who upload videos to YouTube are exposed to sexism and online vitriol to a far greater extent than men are. Nevertheless, guests are discriminated against by racist landlords on Airbnb because of their skin color. Nevertheless, it can be more difficult to book an Uber driver in poorer neighborhoods than in wealthy ones.

If you ask tech companies about their opinions on this, or ask them to expound on how they influence society, only vague and defensive responses will be forthcoming. They say that their platforms are purely recreational, simply about couch surfing or carpooling. They speak of the opportunities they offer people for self-expression or to earn an extra buck, or talk about how their services contribute to reducing the number of vehicles on the streets of our cities. I have met a great many people who work for the tech corporations that turn up time and again in this book. All have struck me as articulate, well-meaning, and well-groomed people with a balanced worldview and an ambition to improve the lot of many people. None seemed to have evil intents.

Several of them have proved sufficiently open, pleasant, and charming for us to subsequently become friends. When I wrote a column for a major daily newspaper about the risks of algorithmic discrimination, using Uber as one of many examples, Uber's head of communications in Scandinavia got in touch with me. She suggested that we meet so that I could gain better insight into how Uber acts and to understand how Uber is working not to discriminate its users.

We met over coffee, and I allowed myself to be charmed. She spoke enthusiastically of Uber's vision, of their many different services (many in the test phase), and displayed beautiful graphs showing how Uber is used as a supplement to the subway in some cities, and how economically underprivileged districts of Paris have as many Uber journeys as the most well-healed arrondissements in the city center. She also explained how they make data available to urban planners, who, thereby, gain a better understanding of the traffic flow in their cities. It was all very fascinating and I don't remember if I asked a single critical question or not. Since we later became Facebook friends, I probably didn't.

As a journalist, I'm not much of an interrogator. The really relevant follow-up questions seldom come to me until after the interview, on the way down the stairs from the office. In other words, I know all about *l'esprit de escallier*, as the French call this. Putting people on the spot is not my forte. My interest in technology and my curiosity make me inclined to be sucked in by the optimism of tech companies, charmed by their vision, and left clandestinely longing to be part of some rapidly growing corporation, working in an office with a ping pong table and conference rooms named after world metropolises. On the other hand, those I interview may see me as well-informed and perhaps reveal more about themselves and their company than planned, something I can use to my advantage. I recall one Facebook employee proudly describing the company as a start-up that naturally makes the occasional mistake. It was not until later that I realized the inherent falsehood: Facebook can hardly be described as a start-up anymore! At the end of June 2017, Mark Zuckerberg announced that Facebook had reached two billion active users each month, certainly a milestone. Bear in mind that on its inception in 2004, "the facebook" was solely intended as a service for Harvard students. Never before in human history has any discovery, technology, or service affected so many people so quickly. Growth in total users exceeds the Internet itself or ancient technological achievements such as television, movies, or radio. Facebook has grown with record speed to reach record size. Shouldn't they have simultaneously learned a record amount? Doesn't their record audience also imply record levels of responsibility?

As the historian Melvin Kranzberg has noted: "Technology is neither good nor bad; nor is it neutral." That tech companies maintain the perception that their platforms are neutral makes them blind to their own influence on their users, and that scares me. What differentiates the filter bubbles created by their platforms from those you choose to inhabit is the fact that you have not chosen them. Were you to obtain a firearms license, subscribe to *the New York-*

er, join a right-wing political party, buy an apartment in Shanghai's most expensive quarter, or begin to watch Fox News, you would have some notion that any one of these actions would inevitably affect you in some manner. When you created an account on one of these platforms, your only thought was presumably that it would make life easier – not that it would change your worldview. Novelist Gustav Flaubert remained skeptical about trains as he believed that railroads would make it possible for more people to move around, meet, and indulge in idiocy. Perhaps society would have benefited from more people adopting Mr. Flaubert's misanthropic attitude and applying it to Facebook.

Algorithms follow code in the same logical and predictable way that trains follow rails. *How* things are coded thus makes a big difference. If, as professor of law Lawrence Lessling has declared: "Code is law," it is important to locate these algorithm-driven platforms in a broader context. Mr. Zuckerberg and many other entrepreneurs behind the platforms we use speak of their contribution to creating a new world in which information flows and people are interconnected. Paradoxically enough, they talk about empowering people without acknowledging that they themselves have any influence. And yet, who has more power than those that bestow influence on others?

To see these platforms as part of a greater whole is a broader issue than simply trying to understand the worldview of Facebook's and Google's programmers. It is about understanding their power and influence and rejecting the tech companies' defensive reasoning that they *only* provide platforms, are *only* engaged in technology, or that technology can in some way be neutral.

When I speak about *our* role in this, I mean both you and I as users and those of us who work as journalists. As users, we must begin to discuss the trust we so carelessly bestow on these companies and how their algorithms influence our own worldview. As journalists, we need to recognize just how blind we have been to the influence tech companies have on societal development. For far too long, coverage of Alphabet (owner of Google), Amazon, Apple, Facebook, and Twitter has been left to journalists specialized in technology instead of allowing other types of journalists to cover them as the societal institutions they have become. And remember, these are institutions whose power and influence exceed that of *all* other institutions humanity has previously experienced. As they themselves are apparently unaware of the full implications of this, I am not reassured by their good intentions – quite the opposite. When ProPublica revealed that it was possible to aim advertisements at a group that identified themselves as "Jew haters," Facebook was quick to remove several other anti-Semitic categories of which they had previously been unaware.[30] Facebook COO Sheryl Sandberg offered an apology and an explanation: "We never intended or anticipated this functionality being used this way – and that is on us," Ms. Sandberg wrote.[31] This is astonishingly naive. Like they say, the road to hell is paved with good intentions.

The picture is further complicated by stating the obvious: We do not have full insight into how these new digital institutions function, nor are they democratically run. What happens if Mark Zuckerberg – who controls over half of the shareholder votes in company– chooses to run for political office? How could we then be certain that the algorithms his company uses would not be adjusted to his advantage? You hardly need to be an Orwellian to realize that a critical attitude to all forms of authority is vital, or to understand how important it is that the general public has basic knowledge of textual criticism and source evaluation, i.e. evaluating pieces of information such a news article, a document, a speech, a photo, and observation or anything used in order to obtain knowledge.

PART 2.

A Personalized reality

The 2007 Grammy Awards at the Staples Center, Los Angeles on February 10, 2008 were a triumph for Amy Winehouse. That night, she became historic. No woman had previously walked away with so many awards from a single Grammy Awards ceremony – not even Whitney Houston. Not only that, but Ms. Winehouse won three of the most prestigious categories; Best New Artist, Best Pop Vocal Album (for *Back to Black*), and Song of the Year (for *Rehab*). Her album was full of great songs. *Rehab* reached the top ten both at home in the UK and in the United States and was played with such regularity in so many contexts that *Time Magazine* named it Song of the Year for 2007. *You Know I'm no Good*, the title track *Back to Black* and the live recording of *Valerie* all climbed high in the charts. The album reached No. 1 in both Europe and the US. A month after her Grammy success, it had sold two and a half million copies and was among the ten best-selling albums of the new millennium.[32]

Google Whitney Houston, and Amy Winehouse will be displayed as a suggested similar artist. The algorithms don't understand why, they have simply learned that they have something in common. This also rouses my curiosity, however, for an entirely different reason. I am interested in comparing how the two artists became famous in order to reveal how much our media habits have changed over only a couple of decades.

Ms. Winehouse wasn't at the awards to receive her prizes. She appeared via satellite from London, performing *You Know I'm No Good* followed by *Rehab*. The choice of songs seemed deliberate. One of the reasons behind Ms. Winehouse's absence from the Los Angeles event that evening was that she was undergoing a rehab program for her alcohol abuse back home in London.

When Amy Winehouse's death was made public on the afternoon of July 23, 2011, just before five o'clock local time, it quickly became headline news. Television news bulletins throughout the evening showed fans gathering outside her home near Camden Square, north London, lighting candles and leaving flowers. However, no channel saw fit to interrupt their scheduled programming as they would do when Whitney Houston was found dead just over six months later.[33] Despite her international breakthrough four years previously and her subsequent exceptional success, both in terms of sales and fame, the British singer was quite simply not sufficiently well-known to merit a break in programs or direct news reporting – something difficult to fathom for those in the Winehouse bubble. At the time of Ms. Winehouse's death, almost every American had heard something by Houston, while only one fifth of the population had heard Amy Winehouse since her breakthrough.[34] A bright future was predicted for Ms. Winehouse, but, at the time of her death, she was no more than a great singer. By the time of her own death, Houston had already achieved the status of legend, with more chart-topping hits than any other female artist. And for news channels to interrupt their broadcasts to announce a person's death, that person must at the very least be a legend.

Is the media landscape now simply so fragmented that it is no longer capable of creating legends? In the future, will we be able to mourn the passing of a great artist collectively as we have done up until now?

The tabloids and their contemporary colleagues on gossip websites wrote a good deal about both Whitney Houston and Amy Winehouse and their, to say the least, famously chaotic off-stage private lives. Both had appeared in public the worse for wear due to drugs and alcohol. Just as the music critics of the morning newspaper compared Ms. Houston and Ms. Winehouse for their fantastic voices, so the gossip columnists and paparazzi of the tabloid press wallowed in the singers' attempts to bring order to their personal lives. They were given a final common denominator; the addiction that killed both Ms. Houston (a cocktail of drugs) and Ms. Winehouse (alcohol). Could Amy Winehouse have become as great a legend as Whitney Houston had she lived as long? An excellent topic for a readers' poll. The answer, in all likelihood, is no. Even if Ms. Winehouse had succeeded in repeating Ms. Houston's achievement[35] of seven consecutive Billboard number ones – the chart that is a prerequisite for global success – and even if Amy Winehouse had dominated radio in the way Whitney Houston did, the answer would have remained no.

Ms. Houston made her name in an era when "everyone" read, listened to, and watched the same things. An artist's breakthrough could lead to overnight fame. This is no longer the case. Today, an artist like Amy Winehouse must breakthrough again and again, one bubble at a time.

Media habits have changed

It's easy to overestimate how much things can change in one year but underestimate how much they can change in three. Media habits are an obvious example of this. Let's take how Whitney Houston made her breakthrough as an illustration. For the sake of clarity, I have indicated everything that might be seen as strange from today's perspective with an exclamation point.

Her breakthrough came in 1983, with an appearance on the Merv Griffin Show. This was a broad entertainment show that was largely unchanged since it was first broadcast 21 years earlier (!). Twenty-year-old Houston had no song of her own to promote (!) but was still invited onto the show (!). She chose to perform a song from a musical (!) and an Aretha Franklin medley (!), together with her mother[36] (!!!). And strangest of all, in 1983, this was considered perfectly normal.

Two years later, Whitney Houston released her eponymous debut album. It was praised by influential critics in *Rolling Stone* and the *New York Times* and produced a number of hit singles in the US and Europe. The most successful of these was *How Will I Know*, which received regular airplay on radio and MTV. In other words, Ms. Houston appeared on all channels for discovering new music in 1985, and repeatedly at that.

So much has changed! The idea of an unknown performer guesting on primetime television, simply because the producer thought she had a beautiful voice now seems absurd (not to mention allowing her to duet with her mother). And who would have the patience to wait two years between a first television appearance and a first single? Of course, the time when everyone watched the same television program is long gone. The opinions of critics no longer weigh as heavily. Radio has been partially replaced by music podcasts and streaming. MTV has lost the status the channel enjoyed in 1985.

One of the most comprehensive studies of worldwide media habits was carried out in Sweden and clearly illustrates how media consumption has changed over time. The study shows the use of various types of media among Swedes in the age range 9-79 on an average day in 1979 and

2016. With a few exceptions, radio was the most popular medium from the beginning of the 1980s until 2004, followed by television, listening to music, daily newspapers, and books. The first inclusion of the Internet in the study was in 1997. It is clear that this was at the expense of radio, while television habits remained unchanged. Listening to music appears at first glance to be unaffected in the statistics apart from seemingly maintaining the same weak decline shown since the beginning of the 1980s. However, this trend was broken in 2004, and, from 2008 onwards, the music curve has pointed upwards,[37] perhaps as a result of the release of iTunes for Windows in 2003 and Spotify's breakthrough in 2009.

At the end of the 1990s, the Swedish Government introduced a subsidy on the purchase of home computers, with the aim of increasing computer literacy in the population. During the first three years of the scheme, one million Swedes purchased their first computer, contributing to putting Sweden at the forefront of digital development. This also contributed to an earlier change in media habits in Sweden than in other countries, although the change curve as such has maintained a fairly similar trajectory irrespective of the country studied.

The Internet penetration rate in Sweden is higher than almost any other country (with the exceptions of Norway, Denmark, and the Netherlands) and media habits are, consequently, more digital[38]. The percentage of Swedes that watch broadcast television is lower than any other EU country, while the percentage that stream their tv-shows on demand is among the highest in the Union. In terms of the percentage of the population that uses social media every day, Sweden comes second, after Denmark[39].

While there have been major changes to media habits over recent decades, it is important to point out that the *total consumption of media*, has remained surprisingly stable. What makes the Swedish study so interesting is that it measures the total time Swedes spend using media. This time remained relatively unchanged between 1979 and 2016, increasing by only 6%.[40] The banner headlines about the media crisis – falling subscriptions, shrinking print runs, and reduced distribution – are not a reflection of the media consumption of citizens but rather of media business models. This differentiation is important and should be borne in mind when discussing the role of media. Even if developments threaten the business models of individual media concerns, this does not appear to be a threat to democracy as such.

News habits are not what they used to be

Media consumption and news consumption are two different things. Just because we read newspapers, it is not possible to draw the conclusion that we also read the news. It may well be that we are only interested in the crossword at the back of the newspaper. Just because we read fewer newspapers than we once did, doesn't necessarily mean that we consume less news. Let's return to the tabloids as an example. In 1986, the year after Whitney Houston's break-through, 39% of the Swedish population read a physical tabloid newspaper, at least three days a week. Twenty-six-years later, in 2012, this figure had dropped below 10%. Had three of four readers deserted the tabloids? Not at all, they had simply changed their method of obtaining the content. In fact, the figure for those reading a tabloid at least three times days per week had increased by 2012, to 42%. Where-as in 1986 all reading took place on paper, today the vast majority read the tabloids' online editions.[41]

In practice, logic suggests that news consumption fol-lows media consumption. You simply look for news con-tent on the media where you are active. One of the largest studies of news consumption in different countries is pub-lished in a report from the Reuters Institute for the Study of Journalism at Oxford University. Looking through the report and comparing curves showing news consumption in various countries over the past year, it is surprising how similar the lines are.

Clearly, there are differences. The Austrians and Swiss are still very fond of their printed newspapers, the Ger-mans and Italians love their television news bulletins, while Latin Americans obtain more of their news from social me-dia and chat apps than in other parts of the world. On the whole, television is still a major and important source of news in all 36 countries included in the report. However, trends show that the importance of television is diminishing. In many cases, it is already number two behind the internet. The importance of print media as a primary source of news varies from market to market but is always considerably lower than television and, like television, is declining. These two curves often follow one another, and, naturally, it is the Internet that has grown in importance at the expense of print media. In the vast majority of cases, the Internet is now as important, or more so, than television as a primary news source. Social media is included in this category but is reported separately to show that it is now a more important news source than print media in the majority of markets and, in one case, (Malaysia) even more important than television.[42] An important point to make here is that this shift is not only from one news source to another, but from sources that do not display news based on data on what the viewer likes, to sources where the idea of adaptation to user data is at the core.

National differences in the choice of primary news source pale into insignificance in comparison to differences between age groups. To a large extent, old people prefer old media (TV, newspapers) while young people like the new (Internet, social media). People between 18 and 24 use the Internet almost twice as much as those over 55, who in turn, are twice as likely to turn on the television than the younger age group.[43]

The report lists the individual media brands that citizens in the various countries prefer to turn to for their news (irrespective of media channel). In each country, two or three brands appear to enjoy special status although it is interesting to note that the gap to those in fourth, eighth, or twelfth place is not enormous. The columns follow a soft curve, and no provider appears to dominate the media landscape.

This development is usually described as a fragmentation, suggesting that a constant number of entertainment and news sources have been broken up into much smaller and more numerous pieces. In a way this is correct, as the total amount of time we spend on media has, of course, remained largely unchanged.

However, the major change is not that everything has been broken down into equally small fragments, but, rather, that it is the hegemony of the wider mass media that has been shattered. Certain components of the media market are still larger than others (media brands that many people still rely on), but the difference between large and small has been reduced, and, above all, the small have grown considerably in number.

The total amount of news and music has never been greater than it is now and has never been produced by more stakeholders. This cannot be viewed as anything other than a victory for democracy. It means that substantially greater numbers of people have been given the opportunity to make themselves heard by publishing their opinions or their music. Of course, whether anyone is listening is another matter.

Thus, this can hardly be seen as a crisis for democracy, even if it appears to be in the interests of certain media corporations to paint it as such. The internet, it seems, can be credited with or blamed for everything – depending on who you ask. Many mass-media corporations have yet to find their role, and we consumers have also grown skeptical of them as our habits have changed. Do we still need these old media behemoths? What is their value today, now that everything they offer – entertainment, news – is available on demand and free of charge?

Somewhat simplified, the great change in our media habits is a consequence of our transition from passive recipients of news and entertainment to active consumers. These days, whatever it is that we want to listen to or read generally requires a decision on our part, a click on a button. When everything is on-demand, we are forced to know what we want. In reality, how long are we really willing to fish in the news stream in order to find out if anything interesting has happened? Perhaps we check-out some news site instead to see what stories they have picked up. If not, we open Facebook, scroll through the Twitter feed, look at a news app that summarizes everything for us. Maybe we message a bot that gives us the day's five most important news stories. Or perhaps we simply ask our digital assistant.

News habits have become individual

The radical change to our media habits has altered our news consumption. This change, gradual at first, has seen a revolution in the last ten years. If we define mass media by the large numbers of people it reaches, then mass media is still very much with us and continues to grow. If, however, we use the term "mass media" to mean media that reaches many people at the same time with the same content, then it has been consigned to the past. Not even those we live with have the same media habits as us, even if we do share a Netflix or Spotify account. Everyone seems to prefer their own little screen to the large communal one.

If we visit the same site for our news or entertainment as someone else, there is a large probability that we will see different things, our selection often being controlled by what we have previously read, liked, or clicked on. In addition, the things we don't read/click on/listen to/like, we need never see again. Algorithms give equal weight to our active choices and non-choices when assessing our preferences. This means that they assume that we like everything we click on and, correspondingly, that we dislike what we fail to click on. Anyone who has never actively chosen to listen to Amy Winehouse will probably never find out that her music even exists.

The binary logic of algorithms (like/dislike) can, of course, cause problems if a person shares an account with someone else. A few years ago, my children logged in to my Netflix account and, over the course of several weeks, watched *Shrek*, I would guess, a thousand times (at around the same time as they played the main theme to *Frozen* what seemed like a billion times in a row). The result of this was that when the Netflix algorithm analyzed my user data, it reached the conclusion that I was a hardcore animation fan with a preference for children's movies. The quality of its recommendations naturally suffered as a result, or to put it bluntly; they became worse than useless. The next time my partner and I searched for a romantic movie, Netflix recommended *Despicable Me, Cars,* and *A Bug's Life.* On searching for a documentary on the East Germans' view of west Germany during the cold war, I was recommended *Over the Hedge, Antz,* and *Cloudy with a Chance of Meatballs.*

And indeed, why not? The Netflix algorithm certainly had no way of knowing that my preferences had been hacked by a seven-year-old and an eight-year-old with a serious Disney addiction. Or perhaps it was just that data that should have aroused the algorithm's suspicions. Eventually, when Netflix realized that it was common for several people in the same household to share an account, they launched the function to create multiple profiles within the same account – much to my delight. Now the algorithm has learned to distinguish between my taste and the kids', and we are all shown only content that feels relevant for us.

The algorithm as editor

Let's summarize. Media habits have changed a great deal and, with them, our news habits. Instead of reading the morning paper, we obtain our news online. For an individual newspaper, it naturally matters little if readers get their news online or via a printed edition. Even if the printed newspaper offers a broader overview of the news feed on a purely physical level, the newspapers' websites and apps are, these days, adept at enticing their readers to remain on the site and read a few more articles.

As its journalistic landmarks were more clearly visible, the old media landscape was easier to navigate than the new one. In each market, there were a few providers that enjoyed firmly established public trust. If you wished to remain abreast of the latest developments in Finnish domestic politics, for example, then *Helsingin Sanomat* would be a good point of departure. The increasing number of new providers and voices claiming to be engaged in journalism has made it harder to know who to trust. I say this not out of nostalgia, simply pragmatism. I don't long for a return to the old media landscape; clearly there were always devious and unreliable newspapers, and even the major news providers occasionally led their readers or viewers astray and were forced to work hard to regain their trust.

Neither was there a better basic understanding in the past of textual criticism and source evaluation. Absolutely not. The reason for this is twofold: partly because people in general had a far greater trust in "authoritative" sources and partly because those deemed to be authoritative felt a greater obligation to meet the expectations born of that trust. I would venture to say that journalists then had a different professional code of ethics. To a far greater extent than today, they had an insight that the work they did was more than a job, that they were sworn officers in the service of the fourth estate. How else can you explain why so many articles today appear less thorough, less well-formulated, than they should be?

Of course, these professional ethics are intact among journalists in the major respected news organizations to a greater extent than in many of the newly started media companies that have no need to relate to their history in the same way. (Note that I am speaking not of individual journalists or specific media organizations, but rather from my own personal conclusions based on my own group, such as it is.) One explanation is of course financial. What was once a normal budget for investigative reporting would seem extravagant today. Shrinking margins have reduced the journalistic resources available to editors. Where full-time employment was once common, today temporary contracts appear to be the norm. It's easy to beat your breast about the superficiality of modern journalism or accuse freelancers of not doing their job when you are a permanent employee of a major newspaper. Many journalists have neither the time nor the financial means to uphold the same ethics. When you are paid by the word, as many freelancers are, it is more important to quickly compile the requisite number than to ensure that each one is correct.

The best editor in the world?

One way for media organizations to save money is to rationalize and eliminate editorial jobs that don't contribute value to the reader. To an outsider, it may seem strange that one of the first jobs to be automated and replaced by an algorithm is the editor who decides what should be on the front page. These days, it works like this: every journalist makes an assessment of how interesting the article they have written is on a scale of one to ten, states the length of time an article will be relevant as front-page material (traffic accident = a few hours, polling results = several days), and whether it is mainly relevant to a specific geographical area (local news). By combining these factors, the algorithm calculates what news should greet visitors to a news site. Other aspects are also considered. The more people who read a published article, the longer the algorithm will maintain the article's position before it gradually loses its place as newer articles receive a higher priority.

For media organizations that began life online, such as Huffington Post and Buzzfeed, the transition to algorithmic editing was uncontroversial. For institutions such as Madrid's *El Pais*, London's *The Times*, and Helsinki's *Helsingin Sanomat*, this decision was more difficult and was, therefore, implemented incrementally. One of the first newspapers to rely on algorithms to create their front pages was Sweden's *Svenska Dagbladet*. After a few initial adjustments to the newspaper's routines for evaluating news (some journalists consistently overrated the news value of their own articles, occasionally leaving the front page trumpeting the rescue of a cat from a tree), algorithms have left editorial staff free to spend their time on news rather than reworking page layouts. In order to emphasize that the paper's fundamental approach to journalism remains unchanged, editor Fredric Karén has been at pains to point out that only the disposition of the front page has been handed over to algorithms, not the responsibility for deciding which news the newspaper covers.[44]

For its part, *Dagens Nyheter*, *Svenska Dagbladet's* main competitor in Sweden, has played down the difference by claiming that their algorithm emulates the methods used by human editors to prioritize diversity in the automatically generated news feed.[45] In reality, the difference between the two algorithms is probably minute, despite attempts by *Dagens Nyheter* to promote the humanity of its algorithm. Why would an algorithm ignore data on which articles are the most popular in order to push others? After all, the newspaper is dependent on advertising revenue, and, therefore, it is in its interests to maximize the number of page and ad views.

Screens displaying real-time information on which articles are read the most, how many times a video is started, or how many times a podcast is downloaded are new additions to editorial offices. Headlines are important in attracting further reads/views/listens. One of the new tasks for editors is to keep an eye on these statistics and adjust headlines on articles that are underperforming. A headline such as "Celebrity's addiction revealed – you won't believe what substances were in their blood" will gain more clicks than one that gives the name of the celebrity in question. This may seem cynical, but a celebrity's chaotic personal life or ongoing struggle with addiction is, from a purely commercial perspective, an advantage to an editorial office that is dependent on clicks or print sales. Covering a proposed new piece of drug legislation is never going to be as interesting to the readers.

What then are the downsides to such behavior? Can the media really afford to behave in this shortsighted manner to attract individual clicks? Editors hand over the decision on headline stories on their front pages to algorithms. In so doing, don't they also relinquish some of the responsibility for choosing what readers should know about?

Wrongly applied, the effect is a populist press that displays a bland desire to offer readers only emotionally provocative stories they can be assumed to want to click on. Many newspapers have seen algorithms as a means of saving money, simultaneously reducing the number of editorial jobs and reducing in-house journalistic coverage in favor of cheap news agency material. Such a strategy leads inexorably to a point where the value contributed by journalists is negligible. Consequently, subscribers question the value of paying for this type of news. And then there is also the perception that information is widely available in multiple locations and younger consumers are used to paying for access but getting it for free?

That information is widely available in multiple locations and younger consumers are not used to paying for access but getting it for free.

Used correctly, algorithms are the best editors in the

world when it comes to choosing front page news. However, algorithms can never make a judgment on which areas should be covered, which events qualify as "news", and how they should be reported. On the other hand, algorithms can contribute information on how reporting should be structured to give maximum effect to a given type of article, based on analyses of the effects obtained from thousands of previous articles. This is how the Swedish news site *KIT* works, having developed a decision-support system for editorial planning in order to ensure that their content is as well-received as possible.

The solution to tomorrow's profitability problems can never be to do less of what readers enjoy. On the contrary, there must be an investment in those editors and journalists who are able to pick up on the important news and explain how it affects the world, in general, and the reader's day-to-day life, specifically. It is telling that the media outlets that have done just that – insisted on payment for the value they offer their readers – are those that have remained profitable. Of course, the higher the percentage of revenue that comes from subscriptions, the less the need to satisfy advertisers' need for exposure. Instead, they can focus on gaining their readers' trust.

In conjunction with Donald Trump's triumph in the US presidential election, many newspapers in both Europe and the US experienced a renaissance. Paradoxically, the same man who accused the impartial press of publishing fake news, withholding information, and conspiring with an elite contributed to strengthening the position of those very media outlets. The President's nature served to actualize the question of what is actually true. His leadership methods clarified the important role of an independent media in monitoring his exercise of power. With Mr. Trump as president, it quickly became clear that oversight would be required to a far greater degree than previously. The effect of this was a marked increase in the number of paying subscribers to major American newspapers. Following the shift in media habits, a majority of new subscribers were online subscriptions. During the first year following the election of President Trump, the New York Times added several hounded thousands new subscribers online and the increased their digital subscription revenue with almost 50 %.[46]

This became known as the Trump Effect, and a similar development can also be seen in many other countries. Perhaps President Trump is simply the best thing to happen to journalism for many decades?

The filter bubbles of journalists

The major quality newspapers are often, and deservedly, used as a benchmark for the journalistic craft: Articles characterized by factual objectivity, reporting of literary quality, penetrating expert analysis, and insightful leader writing. Hardly surprising when you consider the resources at their disposal. However, the decisive difference in comparison to other media outlets is something else; an unwillingness to compromise on the fundamental craft of journalism. Tips must be assessed, stories chased, angles determined, interviews conducted, experts interrogated, and sources checked (and double checked). Of course, this doesn't necessarily apply to *all* of the news reported on, but it does apply to the exposés, the scoops, and the exclusive interviews.

Without this craft knowledge, it would be impossible to continually produce journalism of a consistently high quality – and on a daily basis at that. It is no coincidence that the quality press has traditionally been overrepresented among recipients of the finest journalistic prizes in almost any country you wish to examine. It is against their work that all other journalism is justifiably measured.

By virtue of these newspapers' widespread distribution, their leader articles are widely quoted and can, thus, be deemed able to shape public discourse by introducing new topics into a country's shared debate. When I was asked to begin writing op-ed columns for *Sydsvenskan*, one of Sweden's largest morning newspapers, I was, therefore, honored. Op-eds are designed to help the reader orientate him- or herself in a debate, assist them in forming an opinion, and challenge the opinions they already hold. A few lazy columns of personal reflections are not enough. The task must be undertaken with the utmost seriousness; it is after all the purpose of the quality press to inform, educate, and enlighten, and its readers can be assumed to have high expectations. Writing compact, thought-provoking texts demands effort and the ability to question situations that are routinely taken for granted, to demonstrate that another interpretation is possible.

But how many people care about this?

Earnestness, a great strength of the quality press, is also its weakness in an age when entertainment is valued as highly as news. Until roughly a decade ago, newspapers were considered a more important primary news source for the general public than both radio and television. We should bear in mind that the term "newspapers" encompasses morning newspapers, tabloids, and free newspapers and that the quality press account for less than half of these.

Even if the journalistic credibility of a major quality newspaper remains considerably higher than many other news sources, and despite the fact that they may be quoted and discussed more often, they are losing ground to other media, as a whole, and to the tabloids, in particular. When we examine the figures on how many people use newspapers in general – and the quality press in particular – as their news source, their declining influence is apparent. In the United Kingdom, a little more than half of the population read printed newspapers at least twice a week. Of these, eight out of ten prefer the tabloids or free newspapers to the quality press. The country's most popular quality daily is *The Guardian*, and, yet, only about one in twenty British people actually read it in print.[47] In an international comparison, printed newspapers in the United Kingdom are doing relatively well. In Reuters' comprehensive study of news habits in 36 countries, nine out of ten citizens mainly obtain their news from sources other than printed material. For younger people, this figure is even lower at one in twenty.[48]

Bear in mind that these figures only relate to the printed version newspapers. As our media habits change, can we still assume that newspapers remain important sources of news, although now in digital form? Sadly not. An American study shows that paper is still the most common method of obtaining newspaper content, at the time of writing this[49] No matter how much we might praise the quality press for its journalism, its ability to provide an objective image of reality based on well-documented facts, the vast majority obtain their news from other sources. It should also be mentioned that, according to Reuters' study, one in every four citizens avoids the news entirely (in some countries this rises to one in two)! The most common reason given is the feeling that the news feed negatively affects their mood.[50] In other words, they prefer something lighter and more entertaining in their feed than depressing articles on the global situation. (Which is why cat videos being so popular.)

This is one reason why sites such as *Buzzfeed*, *Vox*, and *Vice* have become so popular. If they are compared with *the BBC*, *CNN*, or the *New York Times*, their differing appeal is clear. These new providers lack the solid reputation of the old but outshine them in how they present stories in a simultaneously entertaining and informative manner, without being careless with the facts.

When we as professional journalists discuss how other people obtain their news, we must be careful not to take as our point of departure our own media consumption or professional elitism. For us, the hierarchy among purely news-based media is clear. The quality press is the most prestigious, closely followed by non-commercial public service broadcasters. Then come news magazines, commercial broadcasters with national coverage, local television and radio, and, finally, the tabloids and online news outlets.

Meanwhile, the public's consumption is the opposite. Algorithms benefit whatever the public likes and clicks on, not what someone else thinks the public should see or hear. Certainly, you can appreciate a well-researched analysis on necessary reforms to European agricultural policy on *Le Monde's* opinion pages, but will it appear in your Facebook feed? Probably not. What you will see there is a somewhat more light-hearted 60-second video that seven of your friends have already liked, an explainer video produced by *Vox* based on *Le Monde's* analysis that describes both the problem and the context. The factors influencing which posts Facebook shows you include how many of your acquaintances interact with them, for example, by clicking on a wow emoji or commenting. Of course, a click-bait headline and a tantalizing link description will contribute to interaction to a greater degree than a factual headline from a quality newspaper.

Those journalists that despise sites like *Buzzfeed* and *Huffington Post* for the excessive emphasis they place on being entertaining, must at the same time admit that they both succeed admirably in capturing the public's interest. Statistics show clearly that the only outlets that enjoy a similar reach to these new types of news media are television channels – something that applies to a similar degree in most markets – and their influence is waning. No, the new news media are already much more important sources of news than the traditional media, and one reason for this is how they inform.

Filtered news valuation

During the fall of 2016, I spent several months working on a longer piece about filter bubbles. As luck would have it, its publication coincided with the widespread discussion of whether filter bubbles could be a factor in the US presidential race, and I received many interview requests. Paradoxically, many of the interviewers I spoke to seemed to be entirely unaware of their own filter bubbles. "Per, tell us which groups are affected by filter bubbles?" If a journalist doesn't realize that they are also in a filter bubble – just like anyone else – how does that affect their journalism? We have established that filter bubbles can create an echo chamber in which a single type of music or opinion dominates, reverberating loudly. Personal filter bubbles may be part of a larger, collective filter bubble differentiated from other bubbles by its specific worldview. What seems important or familiar in one bubble, may be wholly unimportant and unknown in another.

If, as a journalist, you ask people on the street if they can name a Whitney Houston song, chances are that you will get a positive response. The bubble of people who are familiar with her is large. (As is the probability that they will name *I Will Always Love You*.) Ask random people to hum an Amy Winehouse tune, and positive responses will be fewer and further between. That bubble is smaller. Ask them if they can name anything by the hip-hop group White Trash Clan and, in all probability, nobody will know who you're talking about. The bubble in which their fan base exists is not very large, but we happen to know that many of them come from Staten Island, the southern-most of New York's five boroughs. In that particular bubble, White Trash Clan are considered celebrities, certainly more so than Amy Winehouse and, perhaps, even on a par with Whitney Houston. The story of White Trash Clan is a good illustration of the perils involved when, as journalists, we fail to bear in mind that we are also in a bubble.

White Trash Clan had a brief hit with *My World is Blue* in 2013, according to the group themselves a parody of the drug culture of Staten Island, with its widespread misuse of painkillers. However, to an outsider, the nuances of this parody might seem difficult to grasp. Rather, on viewing the low-budget video of the song, the impression is that the group thinks that these blue pills give a little much-needed color to their drab daily lives.[51]

As is so often the case, those who loudly accused the video of romanticizing drugs contributed to bringing attention to it far outside the group's usual fan base. Indeed, to a wider audience than the boys in White Trash Clan could have ever hoped for. When, shortly after appearing as a dancer in the video, a woman was arrested for attempting to sell painkilling medication, criticism intensified. Consequently, even more people discovered the song. The low budget video went viral.

The group failed to garner the same level of attention for their subsequent songs and returned to the status of local heroes. If you ask anyone on the streets of Staten Island whether they know who White Trash Clan are or remember the strange video featuring a girl dancing around dressed as an elf, the chances are that they will reply in the affirmative. If they are hip-hop fans, the chances are even higher. They would certainly be able to tell you that one of the rappers in the video, Gerard Kelly, AKA Incite, was a respected figure in local hip-hop circles.

At the end of August 2015, when news spread of Mr. Kelly's death, many Staten Islanders mourned him. The 32-year-old Mr. Kelly had contributed to creating a vital hip-hop scene on the island, participated in many recording sessions, helped young people get started by showing them how to record good demos and low-budget videos. He wasn't involved in music for the money but because he loved being part of it.[52]

Following Mr. Kelly's death, many people turned to social media to express how much he had meant to them. The rapper Zeps summed up what many felt when he uploaded one of the final tracks that Mr. Kelly worked on, writing, "R.I.P. Gerard 'Incite' Kelly, you will be missed and SI hip hop will never be the same."[53]

To the hip-hoppers of Staten Island, Kelly's death was as shocking as Amy Winehouse's death was to her fans. As heartfelt as the sorrow felt by those who knew of Mr. Kelly was, his death generated no news outside of the hip-hop community. One article in the local newspaper, the *Staten Island Advance*, was just about all. The national press wrote nothing. The international media remained silent. Swedish journalists didn't write a word. Six months later, the video's dancing elf lady was found dead from an overdose. Her name was Sharissa Turk. She was 25 years old and eight-months pregnant.

Strangely enough, her death attracted considerably more media attention than Mr. Kelly's. Behind this lay the journalists' own filter bubbles. The news was published first by the local New York press before being picked up by both the national and international media. Quite simply, it became big news. Why? What drew the media's attention to an extra in a music video while the band behind the song remained largely unknown? Ms. Turk's death should have gone unremarked, at least according to the classic method of evaluating news. An addict dying from an overdose is a statistic and hardly worth reporting. Such news leaves the reader none the wiser, offers no new perspective on the world. Since the addict in question enjoyed a small degree of celebrity on Staten Island, perhaps the *Staten Island Advance* might be expected to report her death.

Filter bubbles affect how we understand values and how we evaluate what's important. The bubble that an individual journalist or editor inhabits, therefore, indirectly affects news evaluation. In order to combat this, editors employ predetermined principles about what is required to class something as news. However, it may slip the minds of journalists to ask themselves whether things that seem important to them are important to the public at large, or whether this is the result of their editor's inclusion in some type of bubble. The news of Sharissa Turk's death is an example of when something goes wrong.

On March 1, the same night as Turk was found dead, the local TV station Pix11 reported on the event and gave it a local slant. "Woman who played blue fairy in music video about Staten Island pill culture found dead"[54] As we have established, American's obtain much of their news from local television networks. Many editors working at other media outlets in the region may well have seen the news and adapted it for publication on their own channels. Others may have seen it in their news feeds and assumed that it was important simply because it had been shown to them. The local tabloids, *the New York Post* and *New York Daily News*, reported the news at the earliest opportunity. Apparently, nobody in the editorial office asked whether it was truly important or only important in their own bubble. However, editors of national newspapers did question it. *The New York Times* decided that the story had no relevance for their readers who had little idea about Staten Island's pill culture and had never seen the video. They, therefore, refrained from reporting Ms. Turk's death. Less scrupulous editors at other media outlets realized the click-bait potential of the headline and published the story.

Many editors working for large media concerns in other countries made the same judgement as *The New York Times*. Many less scrupulous editors in other countries made the same judgement as *the New York Post*. On March 3, inquisitive readers in the United Kingdom,[55] Australia,[56] Argentina,[57] Slovenia,[58] Germany,[59] Italy,[60] and a host of other countries fell for the click-bait headlines. The articles were summaries of the stories that appeared in the New York local press. They dealt with a woman who was unknown to readers in these countries, who had appeared in a music video they had never seen, in a song they had never heard, played by a band they had never heard of.

We may of course feel that it is cynical behavior on the part of the media to profit from someone's death. However, if you joined me in clicking on any of these headlines, we unintentionally contributed to ensuring that the algorithms will show more articles in a similar vein in the future. Thus, we also contribute to ensuring that the media will continue to produce more similarly cynical articles. Their defense is always: "Well people seem to like it, or why would they click?"

And they're right. Who are we to hand over complete responsibility for the creation of filter bubbles to someone else when, despite everything, the bubbles are the creation of our own behavior and biases?

PART 3.

A Faked reality

Beyoncé is one of the most successful artists of the new millennium. In fact, with sales of over 100 million albums as a solo artist and a further 60 million as a member of Destiny's Child, she is one of the most successful artists of all time. Whitney Houston, one of Beyoncé's role models, sold more records although Beyoncé has garnered more Grammy Award nominations – 22 in total. No female artist has won as many Grammys in a single year as Beyoncé at the 2009 awards. She walked away with six statuettes, including the coveted Song of the Year category for *Single Ladies (put a Ring on It)*. Amy Winehouse, the previous record holder, won only five awards in 2007.

Those who don't believe in the theory that news consumption has become too fragmented to create worldwide superstars need only look at Beyoncé. She has purposefully cultivated her fame to obtain a devoted audience around the globe, willing to pay good money to experience her mammoth, lavish, and meticulously planned arena tours.

Many people were devastated when the news of Beyoncé's untimely death reached them on the morning of October 18, 2016. Three days previously, while appearing in a charity concert at the Barclays Center in Brooklyn, her earring was ripped from her earlobe after catching on something. Despite the injury being serious enough to leave blood dripping down her neck, to the delight of her fans Beyoncé finished her performance. Misjudging the need for medical attention after the performance and despite continued bleeding, the star did not visit the hospital and eventually lost so much blood that it was impossible to save her life.

What roused suspicions regarding the veracity of this news was the fact that it was published not on the artist's official site but on a Facebook page called RIP Beyoncé. This, along with an appeal to forward condolences was followed by a prompt to like the page for some unclear reason. This fake news was revealed as such after only a couple of hours, but, by then, it had been widely disseminated. During the following days, many media outlets wrote about this fictional news, "unmasking" it as fake. The news transformed to meta-news. Many media outlets reported in detail how Beyoncé's fans had reacted to hearing the fake news, about when they had discovered it was false, about how they might have reacted if it had been true.

The truth about biased news

Before we delve into the phenomenon of fake news, we would be well advised to find out a few facts about how journalists work. To the uninitiated, it may sound suspicious when a journalist speaks of a story angle, as if objectivity has been cast aside. However, this is not the case. An "angle" is simply journalistic jargon for choosing a perspective from which a story can be made more comprehensible to a reader, listener, or viewer. When politicians explain that they intend to raise a given tax by 1.5%, it is hard to grasp the concrete effects on people, even for an economist. By choosing a story angle that is to relate it from the perspective of an individual person, it can be clarified. By calculating the effects of the tax reform in dollars and cents for someone earning a given amount, and then interviewing a representative of that group, the journalist can contribute to more people understanding those effects – leaving readers, listeners, or viewers to make up their own minds on whether the reform is good or bad. Choosing to a news story angle is, therefore, a good thing and can be done without impacting journalistic impartiality or leading to unbalanced reporting.

Certain media outlets choose to highlight a certain type of news from the same story angle time after time. There are various reasons for this. One explanation may be that they report for a narrower band of people, perhaps small savers, who appreciate all news being angled to seem more relevant to them. Another explanation may be that the editor has chosen to take a clear stance on an issue, perhaps that immigration is good, and, therefore, chooses to use the same story angle for all stories linked to that topic in order to provide confirmation for their thesis.

Allow me to briefly interpose that media adopting a stance is nothing new. In line with its role of holding those in power accountable, the media has always argued in favor of changes that benefit the people rather than those in power. Those who accuse journalists of having left-wing sympathies in their reporting, therefore, confuse the journalistic mission (to question) with the ideology of the left. After all, the left has always been more critical of authority than the right, which has historically represented exactly that authority. Although this may at first glance appear to be the same thing, it is not always the case.

Then again, there are, of course, some medias that make no apology for sympathizing with a certain ideology and are, therefore, critical of those ideas that represent the opposite political leaning. Historically speaking, this has mainly applied to newspaper editorial offices, and, over recent decades, these ideologies have mainly been used to add color to leader and debate articles. The idea behind this has always been to reassure readers that they can obtain reliable, impartial news from the newspaper even if they don't like what's being said on the opinion pages.

Anyone following the public discourse since the millennium will have noted that it has become polarized, more bombastic as well as less conciliatory. The digitalization of our news media has paved the way for biased media outlets that have sacrificed a certain amount of objectivity for the opportunity to capitalize on their users' inherent confirmation bias, ensuring that all news they report is colored by their political viewpoint. The most well-known example of this is the conservative channel *Fox News*, although this type of biased media exists in most countries – both on the right and left.

What we see now that is new, is that these biased media outlets no longer confine their political stance to the opinion pages but also allow it to influence their analyses of actual news events. How is this apparent? If you want to understand *how* an act of terrorism has taken place, it makes no difference if you follow events on Fox News or a left-leaning channel such as MSNBC. Irrespective of who employs them, journalists in the field follow the same principles when reporting events, in that their account should be as factual and accurate as possible. However, if you want to understand *why* an act of terrorism has taken place, the differences will be more obvious as explanations follow the dominant ideological line of each side. (Left-wing: "The perpetrator is probably a lone madman, so we must be careful not to blame an entire group in our society!" Right-wing: "The perpetrator is probably part of a larger conspiracy from outsiders bent on creating chaos in our society!")

As usual, history has something to teach us. In the 1800s, new and efficient printing presses contributed to the rapid spread of partisan newspapers, at the expense of journalistic integrity and to the detriment of the oversight of those in power. By the mid-twentieth century, as radio and television were coming to the fore, many worried that the new media would reduce the debate of important issues to a series of soundbites, handing the advantage to those politicians who could master the broadcast media rather than those best qualified to run the country. In our own century, with the advent of social media – which unites the written word with the screen and which gives preference to video because its superior ability to engage us emotionally – we can see parallels with bygone times. Every time a new innovation shakes the media landscape like an earthquake, we instinctively look to those voices that are the clearest in the confusion. There and then, before the dust has settled, we have no idea if we can trust them, but amid the chaos, clarity and safety seem to be the same thing.

What is media hiding from us?

Accusations of cover-ups have become so commonplace that the question arises: exactly how much is the media really hiding? A few years ago, that question would have seemed ridiculous – especially to us journalists, who understand the absurdity of the idea that our profession would conspire to keep important news from our readers.

The answer, then, is nothing.

However, we don't report *everything* that happens. Journalism is all about choices. Unlike Facebook's mission to provide users with a meaningful experience based on their own preferences, the editor's goal is to give the public a relevant selection based on the editor's preferences and the newspaper's policy. A music magazine only writes about politics in as far as it affects music listeners, irrespective of the large numbers of politically-aware readers within its circulation.

Neither do we report *everything* about a given event. Is a given piece of information crucial to understanding the course of events or to making an analysis? If so, it's in. Is it relevant to tell readers where the protagonist lives, what their job is, what they look like, their religion, or who they're sleeping with? Generally, no. Those who write to us in the aftermath with accusations of a cover up have got the wrong end of the stick. "Why didn't you report the fact that the rapist has Kurdish roots?" The answer is, because it had no relevance to the story. For the very same reason, we don't publish the fact that the rapist's roots are in Canada or Kentucky. It would be racist to assume that ethnic background is an appropriate means of explaining a person's actions, and that is why we don't mention it. Cultural background may play a role, but in order to include that in a story, a journalist must be entirely certain of its relevance and offer a detailed explanation. Otherwise, the journalist simply contributes to reinforcing prejudice.

We must also be certain that what we report is actually true. Prior to a major exposé, much of a journalist's work consists of checking what various people have said, allowing different perspectives to be heard, and offering the subject an opportunity to reply to any accusations. Facts must be checked, the authenticity of documents investigated, and the course of events verified by at least two sources independent of one another. Of course, the more spectacular the exposé, the greater the need for verification to ensure that something isn't published that later proves to be false or that accuses an innocent party of involvement. At a time when the media's trustworthiness is being questioned from all sides, this work is even more important. I know of a number of cases in which journalists have discovered that several of the documents on which their story rests have proven to be skillful forgeries, and have realized that they were about to fall into a trap set to blacken their own reputation and that of the media outlet they worked for.

Anonymous sources make the work of journalists that much more demanding. As the public has no way to check their authenticity, many more corroborating anonymous sources must be found (two is insufficient) and their stories checked against one another. A reason it took so long to expose some of the sexual misconduct that Hollywood producer Harvey Weinstein was guilty of was the fact that there hadn't been enough women willing to talk about it before, even anonymously. Thanks to the #metoo-campaign, women started to speak up and more men were exposed as having been engaged in male chauvinist, sexist and in some cases criminal behavior. Only information verified from many independent sources can be included in a story. Everything else must be left out, however frustrating it might be. If the story fails to add up at all, then it's back to square one.

Journalism is very much a craft. The tools have been updated, and the results may look different than they once did, but the craft as such is unchanged. And as always, the level of craftsmanship varies from journalist to journalist. Some throw their stories together, don't double check their facts, pad them with unnecessary details, and contribute to creating prejudice instead of understanding among their readership. Those people, by definition, aren't journalists even if they call themselves that.

The editor's task is to prevent this, to ensure that stories live up to the standards the public has a right to expect. He or she is to provide quality assurance, and as the one assigning journalists to what stories to cover, the editor also has the final say about what is to be included and what is to be excluded in an article.

But there's more to putting a story together than a journalist and an editor. There might also be a photo editor who is responsible for how an article is to be illustrated (photographs, illustrations, or graphics) and who finds someone to do that and to edit the result.

Large newspapers and magazines might also employ fact checkers (verifying facts and quotes with sources to ensure that they are bona fide), people good at proofreading (to ensure that the text is comprehensible, the language varied, and the grammar correct) and copy editors who writes headlines (formulating something that both summarizes the article and piques curiosity). Television and radio news, naturally, have similar functions. In the United States, a lawyer will generally also be employed as US law allows corporations, organizations and individuals to sue the media for libel if the facts aren't accurate.

All of this work is carried out in order to ensure that newspaper journalism maintains the highest possible quality for the purpose of maintaining public trust. The unique thing about journalism is that the responsibility for everything published rests with a single individual, the editor-in-chief. A news source without an editor-in-chief is not to be trusted as there is no one to hold accountable.

The truth about fake news

There was no shortage of "fake news" or "alternative facts" in society even before Donald Trump drove these phrases into the public consciousness. Throughout history, people have told tall tales. Politicians have insinuated falsehoods to discredit an opponent. Newspapers have made unfounded claims to increase circulation. One historical example is what came to be known as the Great Moon Hoax, a series of articles detailing the discovery of life on the moon published by the *New York Sun* in 1835.[61]

Mr. Trump's repeated accusations that one thing or another is "fake news" are not about this but rather that he has read or seen something that he doesn't like. To label something as fake news has become a way of avoiding an uncomfortable accusation. Many politicians, athletes, and celebrities have followed Mr. Trump's lead in employing the same defense mechanism. Attack is a form of defense.

The term "fake news" has been thrown around with such abandon that it has lost much of its actual meaning and gradation. When something is accused of being fake news, many people take this to mean that it deals with a story the truth of which is hard to determine. This type of accusation fits perfectly into a polarized debate climate. Whether or not something is true is of less importance than whether the intended audience *wants* it to be true or not.

Is it possible to define fake news? How do we differentiate fake news from misunderstandings, satire, the dissemination of false information in good faith, half-truths, conspiracy theories, and propaganda? The most meaningful definition of fake news is that *it is false, one hundred percent wrong, and was created with the intention of fooling people with the objective of obtaining some benefit.* All other definitions quickly become a matter of interpretation, often colored by someone's confirmation bias. The news of the death of Beyoncé is a good example of fake news. Completely false, and created with the intent of fooling people in order to somehow benefit from it.

The definition we use here gives no consideration to why someone disseminates fake news (e.g. financial or political gain) or whether it is perpetrated by an individual, an organization, or a state. Russia's attempts to influence public opinion and the outcome of elections in both the US and France are examples of fake news being used as propaganda or to create chaos and division. This in itself is nothing new – the Allies did the same thing during World War II to influence public opinion in the occupied countries of Europe – what is different is that the digital context allows for rapid evaluation and that the victims themselves help to disseminate the fake news to a wider public. The French citizens who believed the news on flyers dropped from Allied planes probably passed it on in an attempt to convince their friends, but, if we are looking for a comparison with our Facebook behavior, those who found a flyer did not print a new edition to be distributed to all of their acquaintances. It is also important to point out that fake news may also be benign. After the Mexico City earthquake in 2017, news spread of a girl rescued from the rubble after lying buried for several days. This was a ray of hope that provided a much-needed counterbalance to the many dreadful stories of families that had lost everything. The only problem was that the story was a fiction. The little girl did not exist.[62] Even inspirational stories may be fake.

Bear in mind that it's often not possible to say if something is factual or not. A lot of stuff is really complicated and nuanced with lots of areas of grey. It requires lengthy and complex explanations to say if a statement was false or true, or provide context. But a lot of audiences let their eyes glance over the headlines in their feeds and don't' take the time to dive in to details and just fall back on their pre-conceptions.

One problem with terms like "fake news" and "propaganda" is that they are linguistic shortcuts. We know what they mean, but we easily forget to look for the nuances and carelessly assume that they are simple concepts. In reality, both the content *and* the context are integral to whether or not something is fake news or propaganda. Terms such as "disinformation" and "misinformation" sound similar, the difference is small, and their meanings also overlap. For the purposes of this book, this is of little importance, and the things we are going to confirm about fake news do not require that we take this into account.

1. Fake news is a global phenomenon

Fake news has always been with us and is everywhere. In the United States, of course, but also in Japan, Italy, the Philippines, Hungary, and the United Kingdom to name but a few. In countries such as France and Germany, the English term "fake news" is used – as if this were something imported rather than with roots in their own lands. Memories of World War II propaganda seem to have faded quickly.

It appears that no country has been spared, and the intention is normally banal; to make money by driving traffic to some other site with a lot of revenue-generating advertising. What differs from country to country is the content. As people mostly click on and share fake news that concurs with their existing beliefs, the creators of fake news aim for plausibility. I read an article about two Canadian teenagers who created a formula for success for their own fake news website. They began by choosing people and subjects on which the public had strong opinions (such as Prime Minister of Canada Justin Trudeau or marijuana). They, then, combined these in fictitious stories that were plausible based on the prejudices the public have about the person in question (Mr. Trudeau is a liberal). The first article, therefore, dealt with Mr. Trudeau's plan to put a marijuana store in every town in Canada. This story was read 170,000 times and generated 20,000 likes, shares, and comments on Facebook. The teenagers made several thousand dollars from that story alone.[63] Fake news follows the same formula in other countries. Our confirmation bias makes them almost irresistible. And in all likelihood, some of those 20,000 people still think that news is real and believable.

2. Fake news utilizes confirmation bias and algorithmic filtering

In an ideal world, in any debate, we engage with our opponent's best and most well-thought-out arguments. Algorithms, on the other hand, are designed for an entirely different purpose, to maximize engagement rather than consensus. The more users like, share, and comment on a post, the more people see the post in their feed. And the more it makes the information seem like a commonly held belief or perspective. The other side's argument and perspective become obscured behind posts reflecting our own viewpoint.

In the autumn of 2016, during the final stages of the US presidential election, *Buzzfeed* identified over one hundred pro-Trump sites publishing fake news, all run from the same town in Macedonia. The people behind the sites had absolutely no interest in American domestic politics as such, but had found a way to financially profit from Republican voters' prejudices about the Democrats.[64] (Pro-Trump fake news accounted for a far greater percentage of the total than pro-Clinton fake news.[65]) These sights spat out a stream of fake news, although in all probability these stories did not affect the outcome of the election. Every reader read and remembered one or more fake news stories during the campaign.[66] Even if more than a hundred million US voters got exposed to fake news on Facebook, Twitter or Instagram – the real question is how effective these stories were?

There are studies showing that if an electorate is exposed to one extra campaign video, the result of the election will be altered by approximately 0.02%. This suggests that if a fake news article was as convincing as a campaign video, it would influence the result of the election in the order of a few hundredths of a percentage point. This is less than Mr. Trump's margin of victory in the swing states that decided the outcome of the election.[67]

However, what can be said is that fake news hardly contributed to reducing the polarization of the political debate As Professor Matthew Gentzkow at Stanford University and his group were able to demonstrate, the tone of US political debate hardened in the mid-1990s after a period of relative civility over the previous century. Mr. Gentzkow offers several explanations. In 1994, the Republicans won a majority in the House of Representatives for the first time in 40 years, after a campaign based on market research into the words that gained the most response among the population. The effect was that the Republicans began choosing their words more carefully to distinguish themselves more clearly from the Democrats. Cable channel C-Span's live broadcasts of debates in Congress also contributed to an understanding among politicians about the importance of using plain language that viewers could understand.[68]

The increasing polarization of political language does not, however, mean that society, as a whole, is equally polarized, although it may give this impression. Certainly, polarization has increased in many countries, with possible causes including economic divisions and increased segregation on several different levels. On the other hand, social and digital media do not appear to have contributed to this polarization. In another study by Mr. Gentzkow, it is clear that the greatest polarization over recent years has occurred in those groups that use social and digital media the least (over 75 years) while polarization is the least prevalent among the most active users of social and digital media (18-39 years).[69] This conclusion runs counter to the concerns of many, including myself. Even if social media seems to polarize users' feeds, by showing only one side of a story, it does not appear to lead to an increase in the polarization of society as a whole, even if that might be hard to believe given the current state of society.

Despite this, it does appear that attitudes towards political opponents have hardened. This is a logical extension of the hardening of rhetoric. If a party leader offers a convincing argument that their opponents are in the wrong, then this will, naturally, influence how that party's followers think about the party. This development is particularly obvious in the United States. In 1960, only 5 % said that they would be unhappy to see one of their children marry someone who was not a supporter of their own party. By 2010, according to one study, this number had risen to 1 in 2 of all Republicans and almost 1 in 3 Democrats.[70] According to another study conducted prior to the 2016 election, over half of Republican voters considered Democrats to be more closed-minded than other Americans. On the other side, this prejudice was even more pronounced. All of 70% of those identifying as Democrats considered Republicans to be closed-minded and that they themselves were more open-minded than others.[71]

The increasing level of intransigence and the evolution of a more negative view of your political opponent fuels confirmation bias and plays into the hands of algorithms. This has created the conditions for an entirely new type of media bias – the hyperpartisan media. These media outlets have entirely abandoned the concept of objectivity. To go back to our earlier example of terrorism, this means that they cannot even be trusted to report *how* an event occurred. Hyperpartisan media have no qualms about spreading unconfirmed rumors nor disseminating information without checking the facts first. Their answers to the question *how?* (factual information) and *why?* (analysis) are hyperbolic, misrepresented, invented, and distorted, often with a dash of conspiracy theory thrown in for good measure. *Breitbart* is a well-known example, operating on the far right-wing in both the US and UK. The left-wing equivalents in these countries are *Occupy Democrats* and *The Canary*, respectively. The Russian international television channel *RT*, with its close ties to the Russian government, must also be classed as hyperpartisan media, even if their particular brand of partisanship, rather than being ideological, is based on casting Russia in the best possible light and the country's enemies in the worst.

Ideological affiliation influences both the evaluation of news and the content of the articles published (not only the analysis). If something happens that doesn't fit with their narrative, these hyperpartisan media outlets simply refrain from reporting the event, or else twist the story into a form that fits their worldview. One tactic commonly used by the hyperpartisan media is to filter news from mainstream news sites that they consider suitable for their own audience. Another tactic is to support an argument with facts taken from a variety of reliable sources, such as research reports or major newspapers, without consideration for the lack of journalistic ethics involved in cherry picking from the work of others to "prove" their own theory.

Paradoxically, when criticized for their filtered reporting, the hyperpartisan media base their rebuttal on filter-bubble theory. When *Fox News* (in practice, verging on hyperpartisan) is criticized for being ultra-conservative, their response is that this may be simply because the critic is a liberal. In *RT*'s case, if you feel that they are hyperpartisan it is simply because you live in a bubble of Western arrogance and hypocrisy. "If anyone's hyperpartisan, it's you."

This is very reminiscent of Mr. Trump and his friends among the trolls and racists. Every criticism is met with a postmodern counterargument in which the facts and the truth are in the eye of the beholder. They seem to constantly repeat that, as author Lena Andersson put it: "We are our own facts, after all, everything is a matter of perspective, and the media lies, especially about those of us who have no value according to a Western-liberal establishment that cares only for minorities and portrays us as primitive oppressors. We have our own truth and morality, while you try to force your colonial perspective on us."[72]

For many hyperpartisan media outlets, however, ideology plays second fiddle to economics. They are well aware that articles that rouse strong feelings also generate a great deal of engagement. Fake news is created, in line with the logic of the algorithm, to offer us more of the same articles that engaged us before. If a story appears to confirm something we already suspected, if someone purports to reveal what no one previously had the courage to admit, the likelihood is even greater that we will click on that link to read the entire article on that ad-financed website. In order to earn money, all that is needed is for the site to be displayed for a few seconds. Whether or not the article has any substance is irrelevant. Many "readers" who share links have themselves never read more than the headline. (One type of fake-news site, therefore, contains only headlines and advertisements, but no articles!)

3. Partisan media is profitable

It's nice to have your suspicions confirmed, there is security in having your worldview reinforced; it's a delight to read an analysis by someone who thinks precisely as you do, reinforcing how smart and knowledgeable you are. Therefore, we are both more loyal to and less critical of a news channel that mediates a worldview that coincides with the one we already have. *Fox News* is living proof that partisan media can rake in the cash. Over more than two decades, they have consistently analyzed current events from a conservative perspective. At the same time, Fox News have succeeded in reaching a growing audience that is more loyal to the channel than to individual program hosts (leaving them free to change personnel whenever suitable).

Digitalization has made it easier to exploit the political polarization that has always existed. Google's and Facebook's algorithm-driven news environments have resulted in a) partisan news sites finding it easier to reach an audience on the extreme right- or left-wing and b) news sites being financially motivated to lean in one direction or the other. Of course, algorithms are programmed to offer users content that coincides with their predefined notions. The fact is that an overwhelming majority of all new news sites in the United States over the past 25 years have been partisan. Of 89 sites, only one – *Politico* – can be viewed as neutral.[73]

Hyperpartisan media are also profitable. Their tactic of spreading excessively angled news has proven to be financially successful. Breitbart earns enough to be able to expand into new markets and compete with similar sites in other countries. The step from hyper-partisanship to publishing fake news is never long. They have, of course, already abandoned all pretext of journalistic integrity, and fake news offers the opportunity to further increase revenues. It is economics rather than ideology that drives sites and hyperpartisan sites may even share an owner because of the financial benefit. Both *Liberal Society* (left-wing) and *Conservative 101* (right-wing) are owned by American News LLC in Miami, a company that also owns a number of fake-news sites. Compare the news on the two sites, and it is quickly apparent that only a few words in each article have been altered to change the angle.[74] The aim is not to enlighten the reader but to incite them – strong emotions are, as noted earlier, an excellent driving force for sharing articles. And make money.

Fighting fake news with algorithms

Sometimes I wish I could reset the algorithms creating my news feeds and start all over again. My inability to do so is a problem I want to obtain a balanced worldview.

The cure most often prescribed is to obtain your news from a broad range of highly credible sources; the Australian Broadcasting Corporation, *El Pais* in Spain, YLE in Finland, *Süddeutche Zeitung* in Germany, *La Stampa* in Italy, the *Times of India*, *The Japan Times*, or the Canadian Broadcasting Corporation, to name but a few. Many of these have relatively recently begun to emphasize that their competitive advantage is their ability to identify real news (as opposed to click-bait rumors and fake news) and to analyze this in an impartial manner. But how does this help when most of us use social media to obtain the majority of our news? Journalistic standards are, after all, unimportant if they are not visible in our news feeds.

Many established media outlets have realized that there are two important reasons for building up their reach from the ground up on Facebook. First, to drive traffic to their websites, thus earning advertising revenue. Second, to remind their followers of their existence. This strategy has proven itself to be vulnerable. When Facebook changed its algorithm to prioritize posts from friends over posts from businesses, many media organizations lost as much as half of their Facebook-generated traffic.[75]

We must also bear in mind that Facebook posed a threat to quality journalism long before the changes were implemented in its algorithm. The stream of advertising money on which the news media could depend began to decrease in 1995, when classified ads site Craigslist was founded. Craigslist founder Craig Newmark was not actively seeking to financially undermine the newspapers; this was simply a side effect of people no longer buying newspapers to read the classifieds, a staple of newspaper content for over a century. Neither was Facebook actively trying to financially undermine the newspapers, but this was the effect when advertisers preferred to buy space on Facebook instead of in newspapers.

Here's a fact: Google and Facebook currently dominate the online advertising market with around two-thirds of the market for digital ads.[76] Everyone else is left to fight over the scraps. Because digital advertising has taken over television's role as the world's largest advertising medium, by 2016 the duopoly of Google/Facebook had secured 20% of all global advertising income, double their share in 2012.[77]

Of course, it is hardly Facebook or Google's responsibility to solve the press's problem with an outdated business model that no longer works. (You may feel that they have a moral obligation to do so given the influence they wield, but that's another matter.) Any pleas for responsibility from Facebook have long fallen on deaf ears. The company that has spent a decade becoming the world's most powerful media organization refuses to acknowledge itself as such and, therefore, refuses to shoulder the associated responsibility of helping its readers obtain an objective worldview. "We are only a platform," has long been Facebook's mantra. Even if there seems to have been a shift following the election of Mr. Trump, this idea is still affecting how they see their role in the world.

However, according to a global survey conducted in 2017, approximately half of people use social media as their primary news channel. In Brazil, this figure reaches almost two thirds. In Germany, it is only one third (they love their newspapers after all). In the United States, the figure is 51%.[78] In another study of American news habits, a majority of those who stated that they primarily used social media to obtain news admitted to obtaining news *solely* from there.[79] This is what makes Facebook the world's largest media organization, despite the fact that they don't employ a single journalist. Even though they don't produce any news reporting themselves, they control the news items people are permitted to see – just as a newspaper editor does or a television channel when choosing which programs to broadcast.

The proportion of people who use social media as their primary news source, however, is no longer rising but appears to have levelled out or even decreased slightly. There are several possible explanations for this. One may be that the growth of social media itself has levelled out measured in total users. Another reason may be the changes Facebook made to its algorithm in 2016, prioritizing communications with family and friends over news media content (and other professional sites). A third possible explanation is that people are spending less time on social networks and more on messenger apps.

Facebook's attempt to take responsibility

Once upon a time, Facebook was just one app among many on our phones. Today, it is a political and cultural force with worldwide influence, and, for many people including its founder Mark Zuckerberg, the effects of this change first became apparent in conjunction with the 2016 US presidential election.

Two billion people use Facebook every month, 1.2 million of them daily. This is considerably more than can be reached by a single news site, television station, newspaper, or magazine anywhere on earth. Add to this the fact that, in WhatsApp, Messenger, and Instagram, Facebook owns three of the few apps that can compete with them in downloads and popularity.[80] Or to put it another way: Never before in human history has so much power been concentrated to a single organization with regard to influencing people's worldview.

During the 2016 US presidential campaign, the media reported that Facebook was flooded with fake news that was subsequently widely disseminated, such as Pope Francis' endorsement of Donald Trump as president (false). The media wrote that half-truths and falsehoods seemed to spread faster than facts and accurate information. Clearly, some stakeholders had their own motives for feeding partisan bubbles on Facebook with news tailored to those bubbles' prejudices about other bubbles.

Why did Facebook do nothing to stop this? Why not change the algorithm so that news emerging from fake-news factories was no longer displayed? Why not employ an editor to identify and block the hyperpartisan news that reinforced the polarization of the political debate?

My experience of programming means that I can see that Facebook approached this problem from a programmer's perspective, rather than an editor's. Changes that Facebook makes to an algorithm are based on data they have discovered that suggests that users want a change. The aim of algorithms is to calculate what users find *meaningful* – Mark Zuckerberg's choice of word – and give them more of the same. Every time you open the Facebook app, a calculation is made of the relevance of around 2,000 posts in your network (this is more complex than simply the number of likes, comments, or shares). Their task is to compile your news feed and is, in effect, one giant equation.

A few years ago, click bait headlines such as "Pregnant YouTube celebrity dies suddenly" became popular on Facebook. Despite users stating in various surveys (Facebook conducts their own) that they hated these click-bait links, they continued to click on them. Data showed that users rarely shared these articles, that they quickly returned to the news feed, and that some of the most popular click-bait links contained recurring phrases ("Five ways to..." and "... you'll never believe what happened next."). Facebook adjusted their algorithm accordingly, discovered that users found the new experience just as meaningful as the old, and the problem subsided.[81]

However, the problem of partisan, half-true, and entirely false news was not so easily solved. The obstacle is philosophical rather than technical. Throughout history, the public discourse has been well served by offering a voice to as many people as possible, thus providing greater diversity and a broader perspective. What Facebook discovered during 2016 was that the number of voices – two billion – also contributed to a fragmentation of reality. The theory that algorithms could contribute to the creation of filter bubbles was known internally at Facebook but had always been considered as an interesting intellectual problem rather than something to spend energy on, as an engineer expressed it in a *New York Times* article.[82]

Bear in mind that Facebook's approach is that of the programmer, not the editor. Technology is assumed to be neutral. The user is expected to take responsibility for their own news feed on Facebook. Essentially taking on the role of their own editor-in-chief. This is in sharp contrast to the free press, where the publisher takes responsibility for all content. If something is untrue, Facebook trusts in its users to refrain from disseminating it.

In other words, what Facebook has created is an editorial office controlled by robots and their own readers. Were Facebook to employ human editors and create a system for blacklisting those who spread fake news, they would become what they have always tried to avoid being: a media organization. This would force Facebook to do something totally against its nature – to ignore what users like. In addition, the problem is not as great as it first appears. According to Facebook's own calculations, fake news represents "a fraction of one percent".[83]

Changing the way we combat fake news

In theory, algorithms are a useful tool for combating fake news and preventing it from spreading as quickly as it once did. In practice, it is too early to say how successful this will be.

Facebook does more than simply adjust its algorithms. By working with a number of third-party fact checkers, widely shared fake news can be flagged as "disputed content." This may seem like an unconvincing label, but it is an example that Facebook wishes, at any price, to avoid being accused of partisanship or of performing any form of censorship – either of which might impact them financially.

Like Facebook, Twitter and Google are making attempts

to fight fake news, disinformation, and conspiracy theories using algorithms as their primary weapon. Twitter has few users in comparison to Facebook and Google. However, as a disproportionate percentage of these are opinion builders and journalists, it is Twitter that sets the agenda. Therefore, anything that makes an impact on Twitter also impacts other channels. As opposed to Facebook, which requires that users use their real names, Twitter both allows the creation of anonymous accounts and has functions that allow remote control. By using various tools that are both cheap and easy to use, it is easy to create an army of Twitter bots. These are accounts that appear real but that are controlled by one person, and this can give the impression of creating a storm of public interest on a topic. If Facebook's problem is fake news, then Twitter's is fake users. Twitter takes this problem seriously and has created an algorithm to discover bot-based manipulation of debates, although how effective this is remains unclear.[84]

Google has also reacted by giving fact checking a more prominent role in compiling its search results. By supporting initiatives such as "Share the Facts" they have made it easier to verify facts through a search. You can even ask your assistant (if you have Alexa anyway) questions such as: "Is it true that 300,000 Florida residents have lost their dental insurance because of Obamacare?" and you will be provided with a fact-checked answer.

Another Google initiative aims to combat radicalization due to online propaganda. By identifying people actively searching for content published by extremists on YouTube, it is possible to lead them to content offering a different perspective, content that might prick a hole in their bubble. Facebook has carried out tests to the same end. Artificial intelligence is learning to differentiate between news on terrorism and actual terrorist propaganda so that Facebook can quickly block users utilizing the platform to recruit terrorists.

The importance of understanding how media works

To us as journalists, these principles are self-evident. However, for those who exist outside of the journalistic bubble, this is not the case.

It can be difficult for the untrained eye to differentiate between a cheap copy and an authentic version of an album in a record shop (to the extent that we still purchase music in this way). The same applies to journalism. The reader doesn't see how much work goes into creating an article, the efforts in vain, the interviews that gave nothing of worth, the accusations proved to be unfounded, the material removed because it could not be verified, or information that remained unpublished because it was not relevant to the reader's understanding of the story.

Despite this, I assume that most people would be able to rank the trustworthiness of various printed newspapers. At one end of the scale are the supermarket tabloids, their flimsy paper filled mainly with fake news and headlines such as "Standup comedian contacts dead father." We instinctively understand that these stories are untrue, but they remain entertaining nonetheless. Then come the weekly celebrity gossip magazines with their glossy paper, half-truths, and insinuations. The mainstream tabloids come next, with their tendency towards wildly skewed block headlines. When it comes to the broadsheets, we assume that we can rely on their factual headlines and everything they write to some degree. Finally, at the other end of the scale is the academic specialist press in which everything written is meticulously peer-reviewed before the article is given a long, explanatory headline, and functional graphic form without any frills.

My point is that we have learned to judge the credibility of print media by giving consideration to the type of publication, how headlines are formed, and the page layout. Even if we don't understand how much work goes into an article, we can still use these visual markers as a guide for separating truth and lies.

When using digital media, this is considerably more difficult. Truth and lies look exactly the same on Google's search results. Presented in blue headings, black summaries, green links – irrespective of content. The order results are presented in bears no relation to the level of truth, simply to popularity. A popular lie will be ranked higher than an unpopular truth. A link on Facebook will look almost identical whether it comes from hyperpartisan *The Canary* or from *The Times* in London. The only clue is who shared it, in all likelihood someone who shares your beliefs given that the algorithm ensures that you primarily see content you like.

When you're using voice to interact with technology, it becomes even harder to separate fact from fiction. Voice recognition makes life simpler since its easier and more intuitive to say what you want, rather than to type it on a keyboard. In order for this interaction to feel natural to us, we need to feel that we're interacting with someone – an assistant like Siri, Alexa or Cortana – that speaks in a way that sound human. Since the objective is to simplify everyday processes for those of us who talks to our phone, computer, car or whatever object we're speaking to, the assistants are programmed to be inhumanly patient, to never get angry even if someone would curse at them or call them foul names. Their personalities are forever service minded and helpful, their voices constantly warm and friendly, and that makes us trust them.

The problem is that interpersonal communication doesn't sound that way at all, and that we are tricked in trusting everything the assistants tell us in their friendly way. If you call someone and ask for information we detect small changes in their tone of voice, their choice of words and in how they interact witch us that serves as signals to us as if they can be trusted or not. Listening to our digital assistants, these signals are absent, which makes us take for granted that they can be trusted even when they quote a source that is not true at all.

Without basic media knowledge, conspiracy theories flourish

I once received a long email of complaint from a reader distressed by the large amount of information we journalists withhold from the public. What made this email particularly memorable was that he (it is generally men who write these types of correspondence) presented what he considered to be three items of particularly compromising evidence against me. As an op-ed columnist in *Sydsvenskan*, I was linked to the newspaper's owner Bonnier and, thereby, entangled in what he described as "the Jewish mafia." As a regular guest on Sweden's largest morning television show, on the state-owned *SVT*, I was also part of "the state conspiracy." As if that wasn't enough, he had discovered one of my books in the bargain bin – decisive proof that the public refused outright to pay full price for the substandard texts I managed to produce. I replied diplomatically that, even if he was barking up the wrong tree on this particular occasion, I appreciated his critical attitude towards the media. I added that I hoped he would use the same critical faculties to examine the media he consumed and especially those that designate themselves as "alternative." I don't know if he took my advice because he never replied.

One of the most important ways to establish trust in the media is for journalists to better explain the craft behind good journalism for the purpose of educating the public. 1. How we decide what is news and how we choose an angle to cover it. 2. How we reach the decision to refrain from publishing certain information. 3. How we check, and double-check, our sources.

Reporting on this craft will increase public knowledge of journalism and allow them to make greater demands of us. Luckily, several media organizations appear to be engaging in just this.

At the same time, it is vital that we as journalists also realize that we are not immune to filter bubbles but rather are just as enclosed by them as everyone else. When my essay on filter bubbles was published in 2016 (the seed from which this book grew) I was asked in interviews to answer the question of which groups were most affected by filter bubbles, as if my journalistic colleagues and I were somehow immune. Just how journalists can unwittingly find themselves in a bubble was demonstrated by a segment in Sweden's most prestigious TV news program, *Aktuellt*. "Mr. Grankvist has written an essay on filter bubbles and how they affect our daily lives," said the show's host in her introduction to the segment, but she didn't introduce me in any further detail. This was not because I am famous enough to need no introduction, far from it, but rather because the presenter knew who I was, having met me previously on *SVT's* morning show. In *her* bubble, I was well known.

Journalists too may need a reminder about how worldviews are manipulated by algorithms. We are not necessarily objective as individuals simply because we know how to create objective journalism. It is, therefore, important that we too realize that we are influenced by the same confirmation bias as everyone else, sometimes seeing things as we wish them to be rather than as they are. Journalists too live in a filter bubble.

A little more humility would go a long way. We journalists should admit that we don't have an exclusive when it comes to the truth. We should admit that we can be wrong from time to time. A great many of us underestimated Donald Trump, and we should ask ourselves what we can learn from this. We should also take conspiracy theories seriously, no matter how idiotic they appear. The accusation that the media had colluded in underreporting the death toll of the Grenfell Tower fire in London in June 2017 was so absurd as to be ignored by the majority of the press when it first surfaced. This caused the rumor to grow to unforeseen proportions, with resulting damage to trust in the media. Journalists should address conspiracy theories such as the pizzagate story directly – irrespective of whether they involve the media itself or not – in order to nip them in the bud.

For around the corner await greater challenges for journalists who hope to separate fact from fiction. First of all, we have the basic and prevalent use of real photos and videos with alternative headlines, shown without context. As when two teenagers in the Netherlands were captured on tape fighting, later falsely labeled as a Muslim migrant attack on a Dutch boy and eventually retweeted by Mr.

Trump.[85] By the time journalists had uncovered the context and the truth, the video was already being shared by thousands of people and seen by millions.

Then we have completely fabricated photos and videos. Fake images, manipulated using software such as Adobe Photoshop to recreate events that never happened, are tools of the industry that manufactures fake news. Adobe is also working on software that can manipulate recorded speech to alter what someone is saying or create entirely new statements using the person's voice.[86] In other words, Photoshop for audio. Other companies are working to produce technologies that make it possible to digitally recreate someone's face using AI analysis of old photographs. The purpose of this is to create a digital mask that can be used in real time, with facial expressions controlled by the wearer's face muscles.[87]

Combine these two technologies and you can create a video in which, for example, Barack Obama appears to make a highly controversial remark. I have seen some early examples of what this might look like, and, although picture quality has yet to reach the level of hyperrealism, the voice was near enough perfect to provide a convincing overall impression. This type of fake audio and video is something that editors will need to be able to uncover if they are to avoid spreading fake news or running the risk of losing their own credibility. (No doubt will this also be used to trick media to take bait of fabrication, in order to de-legitimize them.) You can also imagine the fallout from a faked, hyperrealistic video that perhaps shows a conversation during which the Russian President and Italian Prime Minister collude to rig an election.

However, the greatest danger may not be that something hyperrealistic can be created but rather that the existence of this new technology will allow people to claim that that evidence of something real is fake. If this technology had been available in the fall 2016, when a video of Donald Trump's coarse and misogynistic comments on women came to light during the final stages of the presidential campaign, despite it being genuine, he would have been able to instantly dismiss the whole thing as a fake. (At the time of writing this, Mr. Trump has started to deny it is his voice on the recording.)

The media's role as the champion of fact

Seen historically, news media has avoided calling statements "lies," even when they clearly lack any basis in reality or go against known facts. The reason for this is that the word "lie" implies that the person disseminating the false information has not simply made a mistake but has made a conscious decision to do so. Since this is difficult to prove, journalists tend to prefer to point out the error and leave the reader, listener, or viewer to make their own judgement of whether the person in question is lying or not.

One of the many things that distinguished Donald Trump's presidential campaign from those of every previous candidate was his proclivity to repeat information that he could reasonably have been expected to know was untrue. Yet Mr. Trump continued to spread this false information. As a result, the *New York Times* decided to begin calling Mr. Trump's statements "lies" when they clearly departed from facts that Mr. Trump himself knew to be true.

In addition to the media's responsibility for reporting current events, it also has a responsibility to create a constructive debate about the future. I don't believe that politicians should be given a platform to talk about the future without forcing them to explicitly state both the facts on which their visions are founded and the facts they intend to use to measure the extent to which their visions are realized.

The thing about facts is that we need them to demonstrate that we're getting somewhere as a society. One sign that facts have lost their meaning in the public discourse is the high level of nostalgia among politicians. If you don't talk about ideology or the future, facts are redundant. The task of the media is to demand answers from those politicians who celebrate a bygone age when their country was great. Exactly *when* was this? Exactly *what* was better? On what *facts* do you base your conclusions? And how will today's figures be altered by the implementation of the policies you propose?

The problem with facts is that they are often uncomfortable, indeed unpleasant. A coal miner doesn't want to hear that there is no future in his industry, that nothing suggests that coal mining will return to its former levels. The unemployed don't want to hear that it was not in fact immigrants that took their jobs. The reaction is often to tune out, withdraw into your bubble, seek the company of likeminded and treat those different than you as the thread and you as the victim.

Nevertheless, facts are crucial to conducting a constructive debate. The danger of filter bubbles is that we obtain separate pictures of reality and no longer speak to one another. Politics is based on finding common ground to stand on despite differing perspectives. If we are unable to agree on even the basic facts, every attempt at discussion is doomed to fail.

Journalists who interview politicians must demand facts and, if necessary, threaten to publish the story under the headline, "Politician X's vision has no basis in fact." Or to call them liars when it is quite apparent that lying is what they're doing. In their role as the champions of facts, the media must dare to think outside the box in order to penetrate our bubbles. The established media needs to get better at packaging serious information in an entertaining and/or striking manner. The format in itself is unimportant, it is the result that matters; what happens to people's worldviews when exposed to the facts.

Something's not quite right

This book began with my somewhat perfunctory assumption that filter bubbles prevent us from creating an objective worldview. Behind this assumption lay two phenomena that I thought I had observed.

1. Facts have lost their importance.

Because filter bubbles exclude opinions we don't like, it is more important that an opinion – if it is to penetrate the filter and be subsequently shared – is distinct and evokes a lot of emotions than that it is based on fact.

It is probably significant that the two primary figures in the Yes to Brexit campaign, Boris Johnson and Nigel Farage, both come from a background as newspaper columnists, during which they had ample time to hone the ability to formulate opinions that carry the necessary resonance to spark debate. It is equally significant that no sooner was the campaign over than they both withdrew the claims on which their campaign slogan was based, and both left their posts. They were never required to exercise responsibility for the effects of the debate they had contributed to creating. Their campaign claims were not based on facts but rather simply sounded reasonable and sufficiently convincing to the ears of many voters. At the time of the election many supporters of Brexit failed to realize that their filter bubbles shut out the critical voices that might have given them reason to question their own argument.

For example, the Yes to Brexit-campaign claimed Great Britain were sending 350 million GBP (USD 470 million) to the EU *every week*, and that those funds could be used to improve the national health system, NHS, instead. After the election, it proved untrue, and no suggestion of extra funds to the NHS have emerged. As a result, a quarter of voters felt they we're misled by the campaign and regret their vote to leave the EU.[88]

Another example: The day after Donald Trump's inauguration, his press secretary Sean Spicer berated the press. Mr. Spicer accused the media of purposely spreading lies about the number of people who attended the inauguration. According to Mr. Spicer, the number of attendees was greater than at any previous US president's inauguration. This was untrue. The previous day, comparison pictures were widely published in the press clearly showing the difference in the crowd size for the Obama and Trump ceremonies. Among the accusations, the Press Secretary claimed (falsely) that photographs had been cropped in an effort to deceive and that, for the first time, white floor coverings had been laid to protect the lawn in front of the Capitol Building and that these had made the crowd appear sparser than it actually was (also untrue). Of the five facts provided to the assembled press core by Mr. Spicer, four were false. However, the Press Secretary was not lying but, in the words of the President's Counselor and former campaign manager Kellyanne Conway, simply presenting "alternative facts."[89] If you were to pick a single segment to describe today's altered relationship to facts, that interview with Ms. Conway would surely be it.

2. Anyone can be an authority.

Once upon a time, to be respected in society you needed to offer a perspective based on facts or to have a position of some importance to be respected among your peers or in society. Today, it seems all that is required is a big enough mouth that keep saying the same thing repetitively. It is even possible to make a name for yourself as an original thinker simply by pointing out that you are expressing what no one else has the courage to say, or that you think differently to the establishment "elite." This approach seems to be adopted by opposition politicians in almost every country.

At first this is somewhat refreshing, the radical voice enlivening your feed, but if you continue to like these self-styled authorities, eventually your existing feed will be replaced by something else. This change is reminiscent of the change in society as a whole. Everything we consider to be entirely normal today was, at some time in history, viewed as radical. Radical voices are not necessarily a bad thing. Irrespective of whether or not you like what they're saying, they provoke thought, and, if you wait long enough, you may come to accept what they're saying as the new normal.

I am not alone in discovering these two phenomena. These developments are behind the conclusion that we live in the post-fact era. A postmodern period when all facts are relative to perception, when what is important is not the action but the intention behind the act or the emotions it produces. A period in which the quick, low-context, emotional opinion seems to trump the slower, high-context factual analysis.

However, while working on this book, I have experienced a nagging feeling that I might be wrong. Call it the confirmation-bias paradox. The more I learn about how strong the influence of confirmation bias can be, the less sure I become about my own theory. There's something not quite right with my assumption about the effects of filter bubbles. Can it be true that facts no longer matter? Isn't there plenty of evidence to the contrary? Not enough that we live in a post-normal society in which it is increasingly unclear who has the authority to create new norms, but can anyone really become an authority and form a new norm? Isn't that a somewhat simplified notion of how views of authority work? Simply because the President of the United States is careless with facts, surely that doesn't mean that the entire nation will suddenly follow suit? It's one thing to be of the opinion that you are an authority, which may be the result of a grandiose self-image. But to be recognized as such by many others is an entirely different thing. Have things really changed so much?

The first time I read Eli Pariser's book on filter bubbles, I was struck by the same feeling, and it took a while before I could put my finger on what it was. Eventually I realized that there was a sense of melancholy vibrating like a distant base throughout the book, something that was also audible in his TED Talk. It's if Mr. Pariser misses the campfire. He mourns that sense of community when everyone could make their voices heard, a time now gone as people retreat to their digital tribes, into their own tailor-made online experience. But perhaps it was never so, even if it felt that way.

I obtained my first email address in 1996 as a student in Cambridge, an address with an illogical construction and endless impossible-to-remember subdomains that I shared with a friend. It did make us feel as if we were stretching our hands towards a crackling fire of knowledge every time the modem did its beeping and chirping to get online. Eventually the sound would stop, its silence signaling a successful transit to another dimension; the World Wide Web. A network uniting everyone. With a few keystrokes, a site on a server on the other side of the world appeared. By the simple expedient of entering someone else's equally illogically constructed email address, you could send a message to that person. With a website, you could make your voice heard.

That's how it *felt*. But was that the reality? Metcalfe's law states that the value of a telecommunications network is proportional to the square of the number of connected users of the system. The more people on the Internet, the more valuable it seems. It's one thing to be able to contact someone, but another to be able to do so in reality. The feeling of true community is in the meeting, not in the ability to meet. It's one thing to be able to email someone and another to have something to discuss. One thing to make one's voice heard, another to be listened to. When something strange appears before us, we naturally turn to the familiar, listening for voices we recognize from other contexts.

There is a longing for democracy on the Internet, and I believe that it is this longing that makes us listen when tech companies talk about their platforms as if they were tools for democracy. But democracy on the Internet doesn't work. We imagine a town square where our voices can be heard, but that's not the kind of space Facebook is. If you want your voice to be heard by more than your closest friends and biggest fans, you'll have to pay Facebook to get the reach you desire.

There's nothing cyber about reality

Something that has always bothered me is the description of cyberspace as something surrounding our terrestrial reality, an endless space filled with information in the same way outer space is filled with meteorites, planets, and solar systems. Another dimension divided from the physical dimension we experience every day. Personally, I have always seen it as the space *between* us, not above us.

I see what we now call digital or social spaces the same way, but our society is stuck with the idea of it being another dimension. "Young people spend too much time on social media!" people say, as if it were a matter of teleportation. The addictive substance in social media is the social – the interpersonal that unites us – not the media. Nobody joins Facebook in the hope of remaining up to date on news in general and obtaining an accurate worldview. Everyone who joins Facebook does so in order to obtain specific news about their friends and a view of their world.

Maybe that's what the nagging feeling has been about: social media is not first and foremost a media but rather a digital representation of the space between us. All those articles and books about the dangers of filter bubbles, manipulative algorithms, and fake news start from the assumption that people primarily use social media to obtain news, rather than understanding that it's simply a way of keeping in touch with people you care about. The truth is that news in the feed invades a social interaction in the same way that someone interrupts your conversation with a friend to tell you about proposed legislation to regulate diesel vehicles in French cities.

It is also important to emphasize that, despite the fact that a large percentage of the population may state that they obtain some of their news from Facebook, this doesn't mean that Facebook is their *sole* source – an impression that is easily gained from speaking to those most concerned by filter bubbles. As it is, a large part of people's media habits is still made up of television, they read the occasional newspaper and happen to catch something on the radio from time to time.[90] In addition, people still speak to one another about this and that, the weather, and the world in general. This all reduces the importance of algorithms in forming an individual's worldview and means that, despite everything, filter bubbles are not as restrictive as you might fear.

When Mr. Zuckerberg declared: "A squirrel dying in front of your house may be more relevant to your interests right now than people dying in Africa," he was, after all, highlighting something essentially human.[91] In order to facilitate day-to-day existence, our brains are coded to give a low priority to things that are far removed, whether physically or mentally. The brain ascribes greater value to what happens to people we know than what happens to strangers, and what happens to people than what happens to things. And, as we have already discussed, the brain ascribes greater value to things that confirm our existing knowledge than to things that contradict our understanding.

The advantages of filter bubbles are seldom mentioned, but the most obvious is that they provide a feeling of affirmation. Algorithms create a space in which you receive confirmation that there are others who like the same things as you, that you are part of a greater whole, a fellowship of people who, in some way, resemble you. For those who are white, male, and heterosexual, all the discussion of increased diversity and gender equality sounds exactly like what it means in practice; you will lose some of the influence you have enjoyed for centuries as part of the privilege that comes with being the norm. When women seize new rights, it *sounds* as if men are losing theirs even if it only means that women and men will get equal rights. For many it's still sounds like a worrying prospect. To be able to leave all that uncertainty and change behind and retreat into the bubble created by your feed must be just as pleasant as sinking into a warm bubble bath after a long day.

And one more thing. In order to reason with clarity about fake news, we must compare it with real news. In reality, the world is not divided into true or false. Luckily it seems we use considerably more categories than just the headlines when judging the level of truth in the stories we hear. Research also shows that people are more skeptical of news they read on social media than on other channels. In the U.S., adults trust the information they get from local and national news organizations by 82 % and 76 % respectively. Only 34 % trust the information they read in social media.[92]

The crisis of faith in institutions

Faith in the established media has been decreasing since the mid-1970s (in some countries by as much as 50%). On average, half of the population of Western countries believe that, under most circumstances, most media outlets can be trusted. Such a level of skepticism is not necessarily a bad thing in a democracy. As author Clay Shirky has pointed out, this new, reduced level of trust may be justified. Were levels perhaps merely unnaturally high during the period when television was our dominant news source? In any case, the effect is that the difference in the trustworthiness we ascribe to a blog post and an article in *The Guardian* is less than might be believed. A critical attitude to all media should mean that the media makes a greater effort to win public trust by doing a thorough job, in theory separating the wheat from the chaff and strengthening those providers who take journalism seriously. As usual, the correlation becomes somewhat more complex in reality. The basic problem with fake news is not a technical one but rather the symptom of a more serious societal problem.

It makes no difference which country you look at. During the past few decades, faith in all kinds of institutions has decreased. The problem of how the media works is not simply a matter for the media itself; it is the sign of a wider malaise. Many of the problems facing Western countries are about who has power, who has the opportunity to gain power, and how that power is exercised. In almost every country that has held elections in the last decade, there has been a populist party spinning a narrative about how those in power (the "elite") have lost contact with citizens ("ordinary people") and how they are doing all they can to exclude and silence those who wish to give those ordinary people a voice.

When faith in the proper functioning of institutions decreases, those same institutions are vulnerable to various kinds of manipulation from anyone from Internet trolls to ideologues, from the Russian FSB to terrorists, all of whom employ similar methods but to a variety of ends.

It is against this background that any increase in the mistrust of the media must be viewed. It is a matter of the whole of society's ability to criticize sources and recognize bluffs. If the majority of the population in a society distrusts what they read or hear, the chances of agreeing on what is true or false are reduced and, thereby, the basis for a discussion that can bridge differences of opinion. Distrust has been reinforced by accusations by many of the populists seeking power that the media is nothing more than an errand boy of the elite. From a historic perspective, the media has been seen as the fourth estate with a responsibility for scrutinizing the first three estates; the executive, legislative, and judicial branches of government. Independence guarantees that the citizenry can rest assured that the media's reporting will be accurate. When distrust in institutions and other groups in society increases so that previous norms are destabilized, it is an easy matter for a populist to confirm people's fears and concerns. Populists understand this. Those institutions that were once able to create norms by virtue of the confidence they enjoyed find it difficult to create new norms while fighting a battle for their own legitimacy. Populists understand this too.

By questioning the independence of the media, populists can more easily dismiss the results of media scrutiny as partisan or fake news if they dislike what is written. This strategy was central to Donald Trump's presidential campaign but came to a head long after his electoral victory. As newly installed president (and representative of the executive branch), the President tweeted that media organizations such *as the New York Times, NBC, ABC, CBS,* and *CNN* are "the enemy of the American people."[93] Such a lack of knowledge of something as central as the relationship between his own and other power centers in society, in combination with a lack of respect for those charged with scrutinizing him, would under normal circumstances be proof enough of Donald Trump's fundamental unsuitability for the office of President of the United States of America. That he has not been removed from office is an indication of something else: the new normal is that there are no longer any norms.

I was wrong

During an interview, shortly after the US presidential election, Mark Zuckerberg said that he didn't believe that fake news on Facebook influenced the result to any great extent. Some months afterwards, he admitted that he had expressed himself clumsily. By not sharing how he saw the problem in the wider context, he had inadvertently led people to believe that he didn't consider that Facebook had any influence on how people perceive the world. In a manifesto published in the spring of 2017, Mr. Zuckerberg's normal optimism about technology was balanced with a new, somewhat more serious – one might even say statesman-like – tone (so much so that a Facebook spokesperson felt obliged to deny any plans on Mr. Zuckerberg's part to enter politics).

The poster boy of social media admitted that social media has its downside. He didn't go into fake news in detail in his manifesto, but he did state the obvious: "Social media is a short-form medium where resonant messages get amplified many times." At its best, social media exposes people to new ideas outside the realm of their usual experience. At its worst, it oversimplifies important topics and drives us towards extreme viewpoints.[94]

In an interview with *Wired* magazine published on the same day as the manifesto was posted, Mr. Zuckerberg explained that the problem of creating a common understanding in society is greater than it first appears and that Facebook's influence is greatly overestimated. "Let's say you can wave a magic wand and get rid of all misinformation. We could still be moving into a world where people are so polarized that they will use a completely different set of true facts to paint whatever narrative they want to fit their world view," Mr. Zuckerberg said.[95] He's right about that. Nobody has unfiltered contact with the world around them. If it wasn't for our inborn confirmation bias, perhaps mental filter bubbles wouldn't be a problem. Let's use music as an example. People have always chosen to listen to music that interests them, and the same applies to choosing news sources. Some of us read music reviews in the *New Yorker*, others prefer the *LA Times*. Some people keep updated on various musicians in *Rolling Stone* while others only use Twitter to do that. Some buy the *New York Post* while others buy *The New York Times*. Some watch *MSNBC*, others *Fox News*.

The major difference between how digital and traditional media filter lies not in function as such but in how we relate to it. Filtration in digital media is assumed to muddy our perception while filtration in traditional media is assumed to help us see more clearly. Both of these assumptions are wrong.

Media habits decide what filter bubbles we create, and the same naturally applies online. However, if the Internet has contributed anything, it is that the choice we have with regard to the kind of information we obtain is greater rather than smaller. Compare today's range with the information we had access to twenty, fifty, or two hundred years ago. It is true that Facebook and Google filter our worldview in ways we cannot control, but you could probably say the same about traditional media, where editors act as filters. Paradoxically enough, it is this filtration that makes a news source useful to us, irrespective of whether the filter is based on geography, politics, or genre. (In contrast, a source that reported everything happening everywhere would be considered absurd.)

How newspapers divide various types of news is also a kind of filtration. Many broadsheets choose to combine financial and sports news in the same section, with culture in another part of the paper. What signals does this division send to readers? Consider if newspapers began with culture articles instead of domestic and world news, as if to say that you must first understand the arts in order to place the other articles in context.

New research also suggests that digital media actually contributes to random exposure to news sources that users would otherwise never discover. In a study of users in the

US, UK, and Germany, it became clear that those who use social media are exposed to news from a wider variety of sources than those who never use social media.[96] The use of social media then seems to broaden our worldview rather than narrow it, as critics suggest.

Actually, search engines don't filter reality

All those demanding that Facebook, Google, and the other platforms change their algorithms to prioritize important news are actually only asking them to replace one filter bubble for another. The very idea that one central body should determine which news is important and everyone should, consequently, be aware of is enough to send shivers down the spines of liberals, humanists, and others who care about the individual's right to reach their own conclusions.

A couple of years ago, Facebook asked a group to investigate the extent to which their feed actually creates filter bubbles. The conclusion was that these bubbles are not as constrictive as you might believe. Since Facebook ordered the study, their conclusions should be taken with a pinch of salt (although more recent independent studies seem to support their findings). This is not, however, the main point, which is one worth considering. Your choice of friends makes more difference to what you see in your Facebook feed than the algorithm, which must of course base its suggestions on something. If you have only liberal friends, you will see considerably less conservative news and vice versa. Of course, what you subsequently like, share, or click on makes a difference when the algorithm calculates what to show you specifically to make you feel that the feed is meaningful.[97] Filter bubbles then are not solely your own fault for liking and clicking on various strange links, they can also be blamed on your friends.

Another study on echo chambers was carried out by a group of researchers with an interest in music. They decided to investigate whether algorithms that recommend new music create echo chambers that in turn narrow our music consumption. The researchers found no basis for such concerns. Instead it appeared that, if algorithms recommended songs based on the simple logic that others who liked this song also liked that song, they actually contributed to broadening the user's musical tastes. Recommendations contributed to users listening to more music. The only negative consequence for range that the researchers could identify was that the recommendations led to everyone's common music taste becoming somewhat more homogeneous as this was based on collective listening patterns.[98]

This means that I have been wrong at least twice. The assumption that algorithms create tight filter bubbles that we have difficulty influencing has been proved wrong. Neither was the hypothesis that algorithms lock me in an echo chamber correct. But what about the idea that search engines adapt their search results to the searcher. Surely that has been repeated so often that it must be true? That is usually the part of Eli Pariser's Ted Talk that people recall, the talk in which he launched the term "filter bubble" and, which at the time of writing, has several million views.[99] It is undeniably a matter for concern if we obtain radically different answers depending on what the search engine knows about us.

When I began my search for facts, I discovered a great many texts by cocksure experts explaining how this worked but surprisingly few references to facts supporting their theories. Most referred to Mr. Pariser's Ted Talk or his book. I decided to get it from the horse's mouth. I got in touch with Farshad Shadloo, Google's Head of Communications and Public Affairs for Sweden and Finland, who explained how it works. According to Mr. Shadloo, Google's search results reflect the content and information available online – there is no hocus-pocus involved. How high a site appears on the list of search results depends on hundreds of parameters, or signals as Google calls them, that the search engine's algorithms use to decide relevance in relation to the question asked. "We never exclude content from our search results, with rare exceptions dealing with copyrighted material, virus infected programs, or obvious contraventions of our general guidelines," Mr. Shadloo assured me in a brief email.[100] Even if I understood that he was unable to discuss how the various signals were ranked, as this is classed as a business secret, I was still disappointed.

This led me to seek answers elsewhere, via informal channels. After much searching, I found someone via LinkedIn, a programmer at Google's search division at their Mountain View HQ who was willing to explain the intricacies (in exchange for anonymity). What she told me over Skype did not surprise me but was nevertheless good to have confirmed.

The programmer, who we can call "Karin," began in pedagogical mode by reminding me that we both want and need a method of organizing the world in order to find the most relevant information as and when we need it. The signals used by Google to calculate the most relevant answers for a given user include their geographic location (e.g. when searching for an ATM) and previously visited websites, Karin explained. However, by far the most important factor in deciding which results to display is also the most obvious; what question the user has entered into the search box.[101]

There's really no other way it could be, Karin told me. If algorithms paid no attention to relevance – how would you be able to find anything online? We would be back to the days of catalogues listing all websites, before Google's search function made them irrelevant. She stated that if we were to replace the existing filter bubbles based on relevance, it would simply be with some other bubble. Why should the critics' ideas of what people *should* see in their filter bubble be more important than the wishes of users themselves? While Karin's reasoning was admittedly sound, the objection can still be raised that the real problem isn't how the programming of algorithms creates filter bubbles but the clandestine way in which this takes place.

There are studies that indicate that a reasonably large part of the population still believe that their social media feeds are chronological.

Karin agreed but laconically stated that the problem is older than Google, indeed older than the internet. Hasn't it always been problematical that people are unaware that their worldview is just that, theirs and not a generally held perception. With the next breath, Karin expressed an understanding that people are concerned about the effects of filter bubbles but emphasized that Google doesn't actually customize results to the extent you might think. Since the search division launched the very first version with customized search results in 2005 and began to give consideration to previously visited sites, new factors have been added to refine search results. What Karin and her colleagues discovered, after many years of testing, was that the search phrase itself – not user data – is incomparably the best indicator for deciding which results are relevant.[102] This may sound banal but, as a tech company, Google tests even the most common assumptions to ensure that they are correct. The fact is that personal customization of search results today is minimal.

The fact is that search engine algorithms are relatively unsophisticated in comparison to Facebook's algorithms. They always begin with a question that generates answers from a variety of sources that you are free to choose from, and in its efforts to assist the user identify the most relevant sources, the search engine displays the greatest possible number of answers. Google's revenue comes from advertising. What does it have to gain, from a purely financial standpoint, by showing two users essentially different results for the same search? If you use Google as a news source by searching for "latest news," the answer will not be a list of current events but rather a number of links to channels such as *ABC, BBC, CNN, NBC, Sky News*, and *Fox News.*

So, what role does the search engine play in forming people's worldviews? In a study of the political impact of search engines in seven countries carried out at Michigan State University, researchers discovered that search engines were a complement to other news sources that people already used. Users checked out an average of 4.5 news sources across various media to obtain an understanding, and those with a specific interest in politics checked even more.[103]

With a sense of academic irony, the researchers note that filter bubbles *sound* like a real problem and that they primarily appear to apply to people other than yourself. But – and this is a big *but* – the conclusion is, nonetheless, that the problem is overblown, the evidence anecdotal (a scientific way of saying not based on facts), and it is impossible to see that search engines contribute to the creation of filter bubbles based on the empirical evidence (the scientific way of saying available facts) produced by the study.[104]

So why does the myth of the personalized search result persist? Perhaps because of the difficulty of evaluating search results against one another. What if it's true that Google mixes paid links (advertisements shown depending on what you search for and who you are) with search results? Naturally ads generally take into consideration both the websites visited by the user and personal information stored on the browser. People are often irritated when they find that ads for products they previously viewed follow them around online for weeks afterwards. They don't understand that this is because they had visited a certain web shop, but instead interpret it as Google knowing everything about them.

So, I was also wrong in the assumption that search engines show different results depending on who is searching. They might have done so in the short period when Google started experimenting with personalized search but not anymore. Sorry.

What can we learn from this? Perhaps that it is important to realize that your hypotheses about how the world works are just that, and that they must be tested before you can be sure that they are correct. But who's got the time for that? And who even knows how many hypotheses about the world a person creates consciously or unconsciously in a lifetime? Our ability to understand the world is dependent on the friends we surround ourselves with – digitally or physically – and the perceptions they share with us. Our preprogrammed confirmation bias is the human algorithm that constricts the bubble further. The brain seeks confirmation that we are correct, and it doubts facts that we find inconvenient. Try then to maintain a healthy skepticism about yourself (not easy I know). Remember the IKEA effect – the tendency to set greater store by something simply because you assembled it yourself. This is true for both furniture and hypotheses about how the world works.

Five ways to change your bubble

Nothing's easier than pointing the finger. It requires nothing of us to place the blame for some minor irritation on someone else. Self-reflection, well that's somewhat more demanding. Many others and I instinctively feel a slight resistance to admitting our errors, to having done wrong, or picking the wrong point of departure.

In the autumn of 2016, I manipulated Twitter's algorithm. My intention was to create two filter bubbles that represented the ongoing debates in the Democrat and Republican bubbles and, hopefully, gain a deeper understanding of the arguments on each side of the presidential campaign. One week prior to the election, I was overwhelmed by the feeling that, despite all prognoses, Donald Trump would win. My analysis was not scientific. It was based on the fact that the debate being conducted in the Democratic bubble seemed very different to the political debate as a whole. Hillary Clinton's supporters discussed facts about how her reforms would be implemented and emphasized her wealth of political experience as proof that she would be a good president. Public discourse, however, was not about this issue.

When Donald Trump declared that he knew more about ISIS than the generals in the Pentagon, it was a sign that apparently anyone could be an authority and that facts carried less weight than previously. In the Republican bubble and in public discourse, the fact of Mr. Trump's complete lack of political experience was considered a strength. Mr. Trump produced no facts to back up his claims that almost every job lost in the US had gone to China. The way in which the United States had lost out through its membership of The North American Free Trade Agreement remained unanswered, as did the gains to be made through a US withdrawal from the Paris Climate Agreement. Mr. Trump simply had a gut feeling that such was the case. (Which matched the emotional gut feelings of many members of the public who didn't have knowledge of all related facts either.)

According to many pundits, Mr. Trump lost the live television debates with Mrs. Clinton through his inability to concretize his policies with facts. However, as the debates were just that, rather than an audit of facts and policies, Mr. Trump emerged the real winner. The absence of critical questions specifically about facts legitimized him, first as a comparable alternative to the other Republican candidates and later as a comparable alternative to Mrs. Clinton.

When his lack of experience was called into question by the press, Mr. Trump countered by claiming that it was this that made him particularly suited to bring the Washington elite to heel. Whenever the media published his evasive replies to their questions on how policies were to be implemented, he responded by accusing them of publishing fake news. While the media stated that Mr. Trump lacked a substantive plan and, instead, merely trumpeted what he believed people wanted to hear, it somehow appeared that he understood the needs of the people.

One week before the election, as I said, the data in my bubbles indicated that Mr. Trump would win. And yet, I had a hard time believing it myself. So powerful was my own confirmation bias that I couldn't then believe what in retrospect appears obvious. I was not alone in making that mistake. Many political pundits were certain beyond a doubt that the election would be a walkover for Mrs. Clinton. They believed that her years of experience gave her the necessary authority. Her meticulously planned political reforms were based on fact, they said. Not only that but also every poll said she should win, they added.

It's easy to point the finger of blame. It requires nothing of us to place the blame for some irritation on someone else instead of reflecting over our own mistakes. I believe that the main cause behind the massive criticism aimed at the polling organizations after the election was the political pundits' desire to exonerate themselves. Furthermore, I believe that the criticism that Facebook and their algorithms create filter bubbles arose for the same reason. New media always frightens us. During the 1930s, there was also concern about the effects of new media. Radio created a mass audience that could be manipulated into a mass movement. As always, the chain of events proves to be more complex in practice than in theory. Radio was not the cause of Adolph Hitler's success. Facebook wasn't behind Donald Trump's success nor, for that matter, Barack Obama's. Yes, Mr. Obama too was said to have been carried on a wave of new technology. Filter bubbles may explain why so many were surprised by Donald Trump's victory. But filter bubbles don't explain *why* he won.

My theory is that Mr. Trump was elected president because the political establishment underestimated the strength of the contempt for politicians that had grown up over many decades and eroded belief in the country's institutions. Confirmation bias may explain why more people didn't question Donald Trump's assertions that China had taken so many American jobs or that the US coal industry could be revived. Facts indicating the opposite are unpleasant, and many, therefore, chose not to listen to those presenting them.

I do know one thing. The American people are not stupid. Even the most frequent readers of hyperpartisan media must have understood that a wall between the US and Mexico would not solve any problems or restore the country to its former glory. I wonder whether many actually grasped the fact that Donald Trump would be unable to live up to any of the expectations people might have of a president, but it was precisely this that proved decisive. The image of a political elite that only lines its own pockets and that of its friends is hardly unique to the United States. I believe that many saw Mr. Trump as a human Molotov cocktail, an explosion at the center of power strong enough to destroy the old structures and force the creation of something new.

Well then. The point I'm trying to make is that it's easy for thoughts to wander off in the wrong direction. Easy to believe that something is a technical challenge rather than an attitude of mind. If we choose to speak of the effects of differing worldviews instead of different filter bubbles, it becomes clear what the challenge really is. "Filter bubble" is simple another word for worldview. When we view filter bubbles and fake news as technical challenges, we automatically search for a technical solution. One reason this attitude is so prevalent is that it makes the challenge easier to solve. Another is that we can pass the responsibility for solving it on to someone else other than ourselves. Or to put it another way: We point the finger at the platform that taught us to click on thumbs up.

Nothing could be more wrong.

The responsibility for changing our world view cannot of course be passed on to anyone else, no matter how convenient that might be. It is something that we must actively work on ourselves. The online world has simply made us aware of a phenomenon that was harder to detect when the only world we had was offline. It is, however, just as common there and is the result of our peculiar urge to seek confirmation of what we believe to be true.

It used to be impossible to exclude someone else's worldview in the simple way we do today. All that is required is to click "hide" next to a comment you don't like in your feed, and you won't see it again. It's important to learn to tolerate other people's opinions. This is both easier and harder than it sounds. It can be as easy as visiting an unfamiliar news site, watching the news on a different television station, occasionally reading a different newspaper. To actively train your own understanding by regularly exposing yourself to contrasting opinions and ideas is more difficult. We must practice looking for facts that undermine our theories. And we must train ourselves to be in the same room with those with entirely different opinions. A lecturer at Stanford University told me that, in her experience, students nowadays find it difficult to come to terms with sharing a room with someone with diametrically opposed opinions. Instead of engaging, they ignore one another. Perhaps they have transferred some of their online behavior to the classroom, she speculated with a note of concern in her voice.

The most common question I'm asked when people hear about my interest in filter bubbles is how to prick a hole in them. As if there were one simple expedient to achieve this. When I reply that it isn't possible, people are disappointed. When I reply that the most important measure is to be aware that you are trapped in a bubble, the response is better. However, as shown in this book, the answer is actually more complex than that.

1. Base your reasoning on facts

Services tailored to a user's needs and wishes inevitably make the user a little more egocentric. In a way, filter bubbles mean a return to a geocentric worldview, a digital equivalent of astronomer Ptolemy's belief that the planets orbited around us. It was fact checking that convinced us to abandon this for a heliocentric worldview.

The cure for filter bubbles, fake news, and skewed worldviews is, however, more complicated than simply obtaining the facts. Facts are mute, blind, and impossible to talk to. They may be false or true, but they are not the truth, and they do not guide us. It is only when facts are placed in context that they become valuable. Only then can we decide if something has increased or decreased, is larger or smaller that we believed and what that means to us. What gives opinions a value, makes reasoning worthwhile, and decides if an argument is worth consideration, are facts. Facts are a prerequisite for meaningful discussion. If you want to be taken seriously, report the facts or assumptions on which your opinion is based. If you meet someone who doesn't have the facts, ask where they are. Nothing disarms a dissenter as effectively as asking for the facts or questioning their sources. Nothing makes a discussion as fruitful as when all parties can agree on the facts.

2. Pay for analysis

The issue of how our worldview is formed can be seen as an issue of editorship. Who creates and controls the filter through which you understand if something important has happened in the world. The business idea behind social networks isn't to filter news but rather to make users stay as long as possible in order to sell as much advertising as possible. The media's business idea is basically to filter everything that happens. They select and report, review and check up on, put things in perspective, and in the correct context. Naturally this requires resources and revenue and, therefore, many of them choose to charge for their services.

There are radical voices that see free news as a social justice issue. The danger is that access to news becomes unequal when people are forced to pay for it. This observation is correct, if somewhat shallow. First, there is ample access to free news, and much of that is high quality. Second, financing is required for really good journalism, and it must come from somewhere. If the media outlets you follow cost you nothing and they receive no state or non-governmental subsidies, then their business idea is not to sell journalism but to sell you. They then earn their money by selling your attention or your data to advertisers. (Which happens to be the business idea that drives the platforms we have discussed in such depth.) Third, there have always been people who have understood that the important thing is not the news itself but the analysis that puts it in context, and these people, therefore, have been willing to pay for that kind of analysis. For many years, the news media was financed by expensive advertisements, but when these moved online, to Google and Facebook, this revenue dried up, and the price for obtaining news and analysis went up. It's no more complicated than that. These days, advertisers mostly finance Google and Facebook instead. By selling your attention and your data, you ensure that you don't have to pay for their services.

I am naturally speaking for myself as a journalist, in the same way as an electrician will always advise you to hire a professional instead of letting an acquaintance wire your house. The advantage with paying for something is that you then have the right demand that the work is carried out to a high standard. With the media, just as with electricians, you pay for what you get. If you pay peanuts, you get monkeys. Clearly you can always try a little DIY, and indeed I recommend it. Generally, you discover that things are harder to do than they first appear.

3. Create more bubbles

Two categories are insufficient for classifying friends. It would be far too limiting to be forced to sort them into either "reliable" or "unreliable." However, to place your friend on a scale between these two extremes should be no problem. We don't have the same level of faith in those classed as less reliable. Their words carry less weight than their actions.

In source criticism to news stories, a critical attitude is maintained to both the story itself and to whoever has published it. Note that being "critical" here is not the same as being "negative," but asking questions. First one tries to asses if the story itself seem reasonable? Is the story objective, or does it seem biased? Does it include named sources? Does it include indicators of time and place? Then one questions the publisher. Do they have a special purpose in publishing it? What confirmation biases might they have, for example, based on gender, age, ethnicity, education? What have they published previously?)

It would be so easy to say that you should stop socializing with unreliable friends, to advise everyone to take a course in basic source criticism or to only obtain their news from media outlets of journalistic distinction. Sound advice but somewhat meddlesome. In theory, things are always easy.

The problem is perhaps not that bubbles seem to appear around us, both analogue and digital, but that we don't inhabit enough bubbles. As long as you vary your social circle to include different people in different contexts, read different media outlets from time to time, discuss various subjects in different forums, you're probably going to be okay. When you find yourself in many bubbles you gain many perspectives while at the same time each individual bubble becomes less significant. If you constantly move in the same circles, discussing roughly the same news and watching roughly the same videos on YouTube, it's time for a change. Take a trip, seek adventure! Or stay at home and join a choir. Or how about following someone new on Snapchat, subscribe to a new podcast, go to a new digital source for news? Do anything, as long as it takes you out of your ordinarily routine. The world is unknown and unknowable in so many ways. The choice is between withdrawing in fear of the unknown or meeting the world with curiosity. Those who lose their inquisitiveness are those that run the greatest risk of getting stuck in a bubble of things they already know and opinions they already have.

4. Nurture your skepticism

Your worldview is formed to a greater extent by those you consider to be reliable than those you have less faith in. People are changeable, and their judgment can change over time. Knowledge also varies by topic so someone who shows good sense about one thing may not about another subject. Someone who showed good sense yesterday may prove to be unhinged tomorrow. However, change seldom occurs overnight but rather through a gradual shift of views until what was once radical appears to be normal. It is, therefore, wise to remain skeptical of other people, the media, institutions, corporations, and politicians. Not to the extremes of conspiracy theorizing, paranoia, or cynicism but just a little healthy skepticism and just from time to time. And then ask yourself if what that person, media outlet, institution, corporation, politician, or you yourself stands for seems to have changed and, if so, what the reason might be.

The challenge is to apply that healthy skepticism to everyone. If you're skeptical about *Breitbart*, you must also approach *the Boston Globe* with equal skepticism before constructing an understanding. A healthily skeptical attitude also has the advantage of helping to reveal shifts in attitudes to various issues, whether your own or others'. (If everyone else appears to have changed their mind, it's probably you, not them.)

With a small dose of skepticism, it's only natural to investigate the facts and, where necessary, look to history or research to understand the context. It becomes second nature to find out how another source or other types of media describe the same events. That's good for both you and society as it gives rise to discussion about why we interpret things this way or that way and, in the long-run, how we want society to look.

5. Lower your voice enough to hear what others are saying

Segregation is a serious problem in our societies. We shouldn't fool ourselves into thinking that once upon a time everyone lived in the same way, shared the same references, and ate the same food, but they did at least watch the same television shows. There was a time when every American knew of the Merv Griffin Show, and many even watched it. The program attracted millions of viewers. Many saw Whitney Houston make her debut. Developments in the media sector have left even our media habits segregated, even in one and the same family. My partner watches a series on Netflix in which I have no interest, while at the same time, I read a book on my Kindle. Our Facebook feeds are entirely different. We follow different people on Twitter and don't have any YouTube subscriptions in common.

This development is unstoppable, but we can actually do something about the mental polarization. A first step is to stop regarding those who disagree with us as idiots. If we want to learn something about another person, we must make an effort to understand their viewpoint. If we want to convince them of something, this is an absolute necessity. All politics is based on compromise, and it is, therefore, necessary to understand your opponent. By lowering the pitch of public discourse and ceasing to portray others as incompetent or having self-serving or questionable motives, we can counteract this polarization and create improved conditions for genuine discussion.

One downside of algorithms prioritizing posts that create a great deal of engagement is that every day we come across furious comments our friends share about the idiotic politicians on the side they themselves don't belong to. The right-wing quote the most extreme statements from the left, and vice versa. In the end, this only increases mutual hatred.

For a while, I simply ignored everyone expressing hate or unwarranted criticism on Twitter or via email. This also seemed to save me a good deal of mental energy. Recently though, I've changed strategy. Many of the emails ended with a sentence in the style of "but I'll never receive a response to this," and I realized that they could also be viewed as an attempt to make contact. My aim wasn't to convince these people but simply to offer a reply in an attempt to show that, despite all, I'm only human and it's okay to have differing views. I also realized that these attempts to make contact offered me the opportunity to gain insight into bubbles I might otherwise never find myself inside.

Those who continued the unpleasant tone in their second email were warned to mind their language if they wished the conversation to continue. I discovered that a good tactic was to write that I assumed the person in question to be a reasonable human being and that I, therefore, did not believe that they would speak in such an unpleasant manner had we met on the street where they lived. This remark made most people stop being impolite and we could continue the discussion in a civil tone.

I tried the same tactics on Twitter, although I had an additional reason for doing it publicly. I wanted to demonstrate to others that it is possible to have a discussion with someone who doesn't think like you do. By changing the language and the attitude, a heated debate could be turned into an informing discussion even when we didn't see things the same way. And you can be made aware of facts or context you didn't know before.

* * *

In digital media, we're all laboratory rats. We generate data that is then analyzed to ensure that we are more efficient users in our big bubbles. Seen through the eyes of Facebook, Google, Twitter, or any other ad-financed platform, we are always potentially productive, constantly connected.

In order to prevent us being overwhelmed by information, we must make active choices, about the sources we want to obtain our information from and when we want to do so. In a few years, we will certainly have improved at this, and it will be both easier and come more naturally to us. The age when notifications cause our phones to illuminate the room or vibrate around the table will soon be gone. Our fear of missing something will be replaced by the insight that we need to miss things. FOMO, the fear of missing out, will become NOMO, the need of missing out.

Much of what it means to be human cannot be converted into data. We can communicate much about ourselves in ways that cannot be converted into code.

The way we cock our heads.

The feeling of holding someone's hand.

The sensations we feel when walking through a park.

"We shape our buildings and afterwards our buildings shape us," remarked Winston Churchill in a speech advocating the rebuilding of the Commons Chamber in the Palace of Westminster after it was bombed during World War II. The digitalization of society has blown apart many of the structures we once took for granted, replacing them with new. We shape our digital world and afterwards our digital world shapes us. There are no public spaces, no parks in the digital world. Nowhere to be anonymous. When Facebook speaks about the town square, it is not in the old meaning, somewhere to address the crowd from a soapbox, but rather the space between various stores, a shopping mall.

Digital media has eliminated the physical boundaries between work and home. Work is home. Home is also work. We no longer need to leave home to shop. In the shopping mall, we are not citizens, we are consumers. Perhaps also extras on a stage or in another visitor's line of sight, but not citizens. All places in society that are not commercially quantifiable are always under threat from the business world. A park is always threatened by plans for new housing, or a new mall.

Over-connectivity means that everything moves so fast. Sweeping plans are greenlit without consideration for the finer details, such as the disappearance of a park. We share an article that seems to confirm our suspicions. We think that key figures give us the full picture, even if we liked the quote from Albert Einstein in someone's feed the other day. "Not everything that can be counted counts, and not everything that counts can be counted." How a person's worldview is formed counts but cannot be counted. Upbringing affects this. Friends have enormous influence. Surroundings also do their part. Algorithms do some of the work. Confirmation bias does the rest.

This book started out from the hypothesis that filter bubbles in social media are crucial to a person's news diet and in forming their worldview. This hypothesis has been disproved. I was wrong. It is said that you learn more by being wrong in an interesting way than by being right in a boring way. I hope that's true. It seems that the solution to the problems that arise from the fact that both we, and our tools, are coded to reach quick conclusions may lie within us rather than outside. Instead of pointing an accusing finger at someone else because you run the risk of having a false worldview, look to yourself. The only person who can change your worldview is you. No one else. Begin by obtaining the facts, then, base your reasoning on them. Pay for analysis that will help you understand the world. Make sure that you live in many different bubbles and nurture your skepticism. Lower your tone and listen to what others have to say.

I'm no longer mad at Spotify because their algorithm is lousy at recommending music. I now understand why. I used to think that I had some idea about music, that I listened to an interesting mix of artists with different styles from different eras. The bad news is that it suggested all that crappy music because I have a really bad taste in music. The good news is that I can actively develop my music taste by starting to listen to new artists. Perhaps I should even give Whitney Houston another shot? Many people who like her also like both Amy Winehouse and Beyoncé. At least if I'm to believe Spotify's algorithms. I suppose I should.

Acknowledgements

As always, in order to put together a book, you need to place yourself in a bubble. In the research phase, you view the world through the filter that is the topic of that bubble. But to finish a book about a topic that is still very much developing, there comes a point where you need to come to a halt, filter out the surrounding world as you try to make sense of it all and, as the deadline comes closer, friends and family.

I've been fortunate in the help I have had from many people in the writing of this book. They deserve credit for what is good about it and I will take responsibility for its shortcomings.

First of all, I want to thank Carl Heath and Johan Pihl. Both kindly took the time from their own work to discuss my ideas with me and to give me their perspective as well as share research papers and news articles with me that proved valuable to understand how technology is affecting or ability to understand the word.

I'd also like to thank Niklas Gustafsson for teaching me the basics of coding in html all those years ago. At the time, I had no way of knowing how valuable that knowledge should turn out to become. Not only had it helped me make several websites work the way I wanted them to work, but more importantly it gave me a kind of digital self-confidence I've had benefitted from ever since. Above everything else, it has given me a deep understanding of the logic of an increasingly digital world that the readers of this book hopefully will benefit from.

Among those who helped me gain insights into specific areas of how social media affect our ability to understand the world a few people stand out and deserves special recognition: Peder Bonnier, Christina Johannesson, Yasri Kahn, Jenny Odell, Bodil Sidén, Amelie Silfverstolpe, Brit Stakston, Ola Spännare, Amir Tehrani and Judith Wolst.

In addition, I want to thank those who read parts of the manuscript and made invaluable comments and criticisms: Malin Bergman, Jonathan Danemo, Elisabeth Forsberg, Rutger Granberg, Jozefine Nybom and Fares Youcefi.

Once again, I've had the privilege of working with a group of people that makes the finished book much better than I could have achieved on my own. The always encouraging and patient editor Olle Grundin of Mondial Publishing, the zealous proof reader Elizabeth Andreini and the ever-enthusiastic and talented designer Miroslav Šokčić.

My friends and family have offered encouragement as well as hot meals throughout the writing process. My partner has, as always when I write a book, proven invaluable in providing objections to observations that I've made, giving me the opportunity to sharpen my arguments or tell the story in a way that is more accessible to the average reader. Last but not least, my children deserve recognition for being kind enough to retreat to their bubbles of YouTube and Musical.ly when their father was consumed with studying a big bubble.

Endnotes

1   Thompson, Alex (8 September 2017) "Trump Gets a Folder Full
    of Positive News about Himself Twice a Day" *Vice News*. https://
    news.vice.com/story/trump-folder-positive-news-white-house

2   Wikfors, Åsa (2017) "Vem bryr sig om fakta" (Who cares about
    facts) *Modern Psykologi*, No. 8, 2017.

3   Silverman, Craig (16 November 2016) "This Analysis Shows
    How Viral Fake Election News Stories Outperformed Real
    News On Facebook" *Buzzfeed News*. https://www.buzzfeed.com/
    craigsilverman/viral-fake-election-news-outperformed-real-
    news-on-facebook

4   "Whitney Houston" *Wikipedia*. (Downloaded 8 July 2017) https://
    en.wikipedia.org/wiki/Whitney_Houston#Reaction

5   *The State of the News Media 2011,* Pew Research Center Project for
    Excellence in Journalism. http://www.stateofthemedia.org/2011/
    overview-2/key-findings/

6   CNN Staff (2012) "Stunned celebrities mourn Whitney Houston"
    CNN. February 12. http://edition.cnn.com/2012/02/12/showbiz/
    whitney-houston-reactions/

7   Hosanagar. Kartik; Fleder, Daniel; Lee, Dokyun and Buja,
    Andreas (2014) "Will the Global Village Fracture Into Tribes?
    Recommender Systems and Their Effects on Consumer
    Fragmentation" *Management Science,* 40 (4), http://papers.ssrn.
    com/sol3/papers.cfm?abstract_id=1321962

8   Mangalindan, JP (2012) "Amazon's recommendation secret" *Fortune*, July 30. Fortune.com (Downloaded 09/22/2016). http://fortune.com/2012/07/30/amazons-recommendation-secret/

9   MacKenzie, Ian; Meyer, Chris and Noble, Steve (2013) "How retailers can keep up with consumers." McKinsey & Company. October. Mckinsey.com: http://www.mckinsey.com/industries/retail/our-insights/how-retailers-can-keep-up-with-consumers

10 Thomson, Robert (06/15/2017) "The Almighty Algorithm – 'fake news' and other consequences of Google, Amazon and Facebook's relentless focus on quantity over quality." *Fox News*. http://www.foxnews.com/opinion/2017/06/15/news-corp-ceo-almighty-algorithm-fake-news-and-other-consequences-google-amazon-and-facebooks-relentless-focus-on-quantity-over-quality.html

11 Ibid.

12 Streitfield, David (12 October 2012) "Amazon and Its Missing Books" *New York Times - Bits blog.* https://bits.blogs.nytimes.com/2014/10/12/amazon-and-its-missing-books/

13 Ibid.

14 Ibid.

15 Orihuela, Rodrigo (26 February 2017) "Telefonica Plans to Give Customers More Control Over Their Data" *Bloomberg.* https://www.bloomberg.com/news/articles/2017-02-26/telefonica-plans-to-give-customers-more-control-over-their-data

16 Popov, Vesselin (5 September 2017) Speech at *The Conference* in Malmö, Sweden.

17 Hempel, Jessie (21 June 2017) "Inside Microsoft's AI Comeback" *Wired.* https://www.wired.com/story/inside-microsofts-ai-comeback/

18 Wikfors, Åsa (2017) "Vem bryr sig om fakta" (Who cares about facts) *Modern Psykologi*, No. 8, 2017.

19 Tatman, Rachel (12 July 2016) "Google voice recognition has a gender bias". *The Hearing things and making noice blog.* Source: https://makingnoiseandhearingthings.com/2016/07/12/googles-speech-recognition-has-a-gender-bias/

20 Smith, Jack (11 October 2016) "Crime prediction tool may reinforce discriminatory policing" *Business Insider. Source: http://uk.businessinsider.com/predictive-policing-disc07)riminatory-police-crime-2016-10?r=US&IR=T*

21 Carpenter, Julia (7 July 2015) "Google's algoritm shows prestigious job ads to men, but not women" *The Independent.*

22 Pariser, Eli (2011) "Beware online 'filter bubbles'"[speech] *TED TALKS.* Ted.com.

23 Goldman, Adam (7 December 2016) "The Comet Ping Pong Gunman Answers Our Reporter's Questions" *The New York Times - https://www.nytimes.com/2016/12/07/us/edgar-welch-comet-pizza-fake-news.html*

24 Haag, Matthew & alam, Maya (22 June 2017) "Gunman in 'Pizzagate' Shooting Is Sentenced to 4 Years in Prison " *The New York Times.*

25 Holley, Peter (1 July 2017) "No, NASA isn't hiding kidnapped children on Mars." *The Washington Post.*

26 Swedish Union of Journalists (2017) Publication Regulations. Downloaded 09/10/2017 from sjf.se https://www.sjf.se/yrkesfragor/yrkesetik/spelregler-for-press-radio-och-tv/publicitetsregler

27 Reinhard, Beth, Davis, Aron C., and Ba Tran, Andrew (29 November 2017) "Woman's effort to infiltrate The Washington Post dated back months" *The Washington Post.* https://www.washingtonpost.com/investigations/womans-effort-to-infiltrate-the-washington-post-dates-back-months/2017/11/29/ce95e01a-d51e-11e7-b62d-d9345ced896d_story.html?utm_term=.bda8db5d37e8

28   Pariser, Eli (2011) "Beware online 'filter bubbles'"[speech] *TED TALKS*. Ted.com. https://www.ted.com/talks/eli_pariser_beware_online_filter_bubbles

29   Ibid.

30   Angwin, Julia; Varner, Madeleine & Tobin, Ariana (24 September 2017) "Facebook Enabled Advertisers to Reach 'Jew Haters' " *ProPublica*. https://www.propublica.org/article/facebook-enabled-advertisers-to-reach-jew-haters

31   Sandberg, Sheryl (20 September 2017) Facebook post. https://www.facebook.com/sheryl/posts/10159255449515177

32   "Amy Winehouse" *Wikipedia*. wikipedia.org (Downloaded 08/28/2016). https://en.wikipedia.org/wiki/Amy_Winehouse#2008:_Continued_success_and_acclaim

33   BBC News (23 July 2011) "Amy Winehouse found dead, age 27". *BBC*. Downloaded 06/27/2017 from archive.org https://web.archive.org/web/20110723215847/http://www.bbc.co.uk/news/uk-14262237

34   "Amy Winehouse" *Wikipedia*. wikipedia.org (Downloaded 08/28/2016). https://en.wikipedia.org/wiki/Amy_Winehouse#2008:_Continued_success_and_acclaim

35   Whitney Houston chart history" *Billboard*. http://www.billboard.com/artist/431329/whitney-houston/chart?sort=date&f=379

36   "Whitney Houston's 'Home' live on the Merv Griffin Show 1985" [tv show] (2009) Dailymotion dailymotion.com (Downloaded 09/29/2016). *Authors note:* There are several wrongly dated clips available of Houston's appearance on the Merv Griffin Show. This clip is from 1983 and not 1985 as stated by Dailymotion, although Houston did appear on the show in 1985, but with a different song. http://www.dailymotion.com/video/xbof6k_whitney-houston-s-home-live-on-the_music

37   Nordicom-Sweden's Media Barometer 2016. (2016) Nordicom. http://nordicom.gu.se/sv/statistik-fakta/mediestatistik

38 Internet World Stats http://www.internetworldstats.com internet population estimate 2017.

39 Standard Eurobarometer 86, (2016) Annex – Media Usage in the EU. http://ec.europa.eu/commfrontoffice/publicopinion/index.cfm/Survey/getSurveyDetail/instruments/STANDARD/surveyKy/2137

40 Nordicom-Sweden's Media Barometer 2016. (2016) Nordicom. http://nordicom.gu.se/sv/statistik-fakta/mediestatistik

41 Jalakas, Andreas and Wadbring, Ingela (2014) "Ska man gråta om papperstidningen försvinner?" (Would the disappearance of printed newspapers be any reason for tears?) included in Bergström, Annika and Oscarsson, Henrik (ed.), *Mittfåra och marginal* (The mainstream and the margins) Gothenburg: SOM Institute. http://miun.diva-portal.org/smash/record.jsf?pid=diva2%3A761578&dswid=9147

42 Digital News Report 2017 (2017) Reuters Institute for the Study of Journalism, Oxford University. http://www.digitalnewsreport.org/survey/2017/resources-2017/

43 Ibid.

44 Karén, Fredric (4 July 2017). Speech at a seminar on algorithms, arranged by Stockholm University

45 Wolodarski, Peter (3 August 2016) "@jocxy vi strävar, tvärtemot vad många tror, aktivt efter mångfald i det automatiserade flödet på DN.se med hjälp av algoritmer" (@jocxy, despite what many believe, using algorithms we actively strive for diversity in the automated stream on DN.se [tweet] Twitter. https://twitter.com/pwolodarski/status/760811773696106496.

46 Ember, Sydney (1 November 2017) "New York Times Co. Reports Solid Digital Growth as Print Slides" *The New York Times.* https://www.nytimes.com/2017/11/01/business/media/new-york-times-earnings.html

47 Report: Taking Part 2014/15, Focus on: Newspaper Readership. (2015) Department of Media, Culture and Sport. https://www. gov.uk/government/uploads/system/uploads/attachment_data/ file/476117/Taking_Part_201415_Focus_on_Newspaper_ readership.pdf

48 Digital News Report 2017 (2017) Reuters Institute for the Study of Journalism, Oxford University. http://www.digitalnewsreport.org/ survey/2017/resources-2017/

49 State of the Media 2016 - Newspapers: Fact Sheet (2016) *Pew Research*. http://www.journalism.org/2016/06/15/newspapers-fact-sheet/

50 Digital News Report 2017 (2017) Reuters Institute for the Study of Journalism, Oxford University. http://www.digitalnewsreport.org/ survey/2017/resources-2017/

51 "My World is Blue" [music video] (16 July 2012) YouTube. https:// www.youtube.com/watch?v=1kOoyWVDNZc

52 Lavis, Ryan (27 August 2015) "Staten Island hip-hop artist Gerard Kelly had passion for making music." *Staten Island Advance*. http://www.silive.com/news/index.ssf/2015/08/staten_island_ rapper_gerard_ke.html

53 Zeps (2015) *Creepin' - featuring Mike Checks & Incite 333 (R.I.P. Incite)* [song] Soundcloud.com. https://soundcloud.com/zeps/ creepin-featuring-mike-checks-incite-333-rip-incite

54 Tanner, Jeremy (1 March 2016) "Woman who played blue fairy in music video about Staten Island pill culture found dead" *Pix11*. pix11.com.

55 Farberov, Snejana (2 March 2016) "YouTube sensation 'blue drug fairy', 25, found dead in apparent overdose while eight months pregnant" *Daily Mail*. http://www.dailymail.co.uk/news/ article-3473376/YouTube-sensation-blue-drug-fairy-25-dead-apparent-overdose-eight-months-pregnant.html

56   Tacopino, Joe (1 March 2016) "YouTube 'blue drug fairy' found dead in apparent overdose" *News Corp Australia.* http://www.news.com.au/technology/online/youtube-blue-drug-fairy-found-dead-in-apparent-overdose/news-story/13106bdf7bb959f57deb016 0860a6b6d

57   Editorial (2 March 2016) "Hacía campaña contra las drogas y murió de sobredosis: ¿quién era Sharissa Turk?" *TN.* http://tn.com.ar/internacional/abogaba-contra-las-drogas-y-murio-de-sobredosis-quien-era-sharissa-turk-el-hada-azul-de-internet_657033

58   Editorial (2 March 2016) "YouTube zvezda umrla v osmem mesecu nosečnosti" *Zurnal24.* http://www.zurnal24.si/youtube-zvezda-sharissa-turk-umrla-v-osmem-mesecu-nosecnosti-clanek-266270

59   Editorial (2 March 2016) " 'Drogen-Fee' aus YouTube-Hit tot aufgefunden" *Focus.* http://www.focus.de/kultur/medien/vermutlicher-drogentod-blaue-fee-aus-youtube-video-hit-tot-aufgefunden_id_5330618.html

60   Editorial (2 March 2016) "Sharissa Turk morta di overdose, era famosa per uno spot antidroga" *Today Donna.* http://www.today.it/donna/sharissa-turk-morta-overdose-video-droga.html

61   Allcott, Hunt & Gentzkow, Matthew (2017) "Social Media and Fake News in the 2016 Election" *Journal of Economic Perspectives*—Volume 31, Number 2. http://web.stanford.edu/~gentzkow/research/fakenews.pdf

62   Campoy, Ana (23 September 2017) "A schoolgirl trapped in Mexico's earthquake rubble won the world's hearts—except she didn't exist" *Quartz.* https://qz.com/1084105/a-schoolgirl-trapped-in-mexicos-earthquake-rubble-won-the-worlds-hearts-except-she-didnt-exist/

63   Silverman, Craig (9 August 2016) "These Two Teenagers Keep Fooling The Internet With Justin Trudeau Hoaxes" Buzzfeed. https://www.buzzfeed.com/craigsilverman/teen-trudeau-hoaxes

64 Silverman, Craig; Alexander, Lawrence (4 November 2016) "How Teens In The Balkans Are Duping Trump Supporters With Fake News". *Buzzfeed*. https://www.buzzfeed.com/craigsilverman/how-macedonia-became-a-global-hub-for-pro-trump-misinfo

65 Allcott, Hunt & Gentzkow, Matthew (2017) "Social Media and Fake News in the 2016 Election" *Journal of Economic Perspectives*—Volume 31, Number 2. http://web.stanford.edu/~gentzkow/research/fakenews.pdf

66 Ibid.

67 Ibid.

68 Gentzkow, Matthew; Shapiro, Jesse and Taddy, Matt (2017) "Measuring Polarization in High-Dimensional Data: Method and Application to Congressional Speech" Stanford University http://web.stanford.edu/~gentzkow/research/politext.pdf

69 Boxell, Levi; Gentzkow, Matthew and Shapiro, Jesse (2017) "Is the internet causing political polarization? Evidence from demographics." Stanford University. http://web.stanford.edu/~gentzkow/research/age-polar.pdf

70 Ibid.

71 "Partisanship and Political Animosity in 2016" (22 June 2016) Pew Research. Downloaded from people-press.org http://www.people-press.org/2016/06/22/partisanship-and-political-animosity-in-2016/

72 Andersson, Lena (16 September 2017) "Källkritiker har vi redan nog av" (We already have enough source critics) *Dagens Nyheter.*

73 Fischer, Sara; Vavra, Shannon (23 February 2017) "The recent explosion of right-wing news sites." *Axios*. https://www.axios.com/the-partisan-explosion-of-digital-news-2279022772.html

74 Silverman, Craig (28 February 2017) "This Is How Hyperpartisan News Gets Made" *BuzzFeed News*. https://www.buzzfeed.com/craigsilverman/how-the-hyperpartisan-sausage-is-made

75 Ingram, Mathew (16 Augusti 2016) "Facebook Traffic to U.S.
News Sites Has Fallen by Double Digits, Report Says" *Fortune.*
http://fortune.com/2016/08/16/facebook-traffic-media/

76 Ingram, Matthew (26 April 2017) "Google and Facebook Account
For Nearly All Growth in Digital Ads" *Fortune.* http://fortune.
com/2017/04/26/google-facebook-digital-ads/

77 Kollewe, Julia (2 May 2017) "Google and Facebook bring in one-
fifth of global ad revenue." *The Guardian.*

78 Digital News Report 2017 (2017) Reuters Institute for the Study of
Journalism, Oxford University. http://www.digitalnewsreport.org/
survey/2017/resources-2017/

79 Gottfried, Jeffery and Shearer, Elisa (26 May 2016) "News Use
Across Social Media Platforms 2016" *Pew Research Center.* http://
www.journalism.org/2016/05/26/news-use-across-social-media-
platforms-2016/

80 Yeh, Oliver (17 April 2017) "Top Apps of Q1 2017: Netflix
Dominated Worldwide Revenue, Which Grew 63% YoY"
SensorTower. https://sensortower.com/blog/top-apps-q1-2017

81 Manjoo, Farhad (25 April 2017) "Can Facebook Fix Its Own Worst
Bug?" New York Times.

82 Ibid.

83 Ibid.

84 Manjoo, Farhad (31 may 2017) "How Twitter Is Being Gamed to
Feed Misinformation" *The New York Times.*

85 Henley, Jon (30 November 2017) "Videos tweeted by Trump: where
are they from and what do they really show?" *The Guardian.* https://
www.theguardian.com/us-news/2017/nov/30/videos-tweeted-by-
trump-where-are-they-from-and-what-do-they-really-show

86 Anthony, Sebastian (11 July 2016) "Adobe demos 'photoshop for
audio,' lets you edit speech as easily as text" *ARS Technica.* https://
arstechnica.com/information-technology/2016/11/adobe-voco-
photoshop-for-audio-speech-editing/

87 *BBC* (17 July 2017) "Fake Obama created using AI tool to make phony speeches" http://www.bbc.com/news/av/technology-40598465/fake-obama-created-using-ai-tool-to-make-phoney-speeches

88 Farand, Cloe (21 August 2017) "Quarter of Brexit voters say they were misled, poll finds" *The Independent*. http://www.independent.co.uk/news/uk/home-news/brexit-voters-poll-mislead-leave-campaign-nhs-claims-lies-remain-win-second-referendum-a7905786.html

89 Blake, Aron (22 January 2017) "Kellyanne Conway says Donald Trump's team has 'alternative facts.' Which pretty much says it all." *Washington Post*. https://www.washingtonpost.com/news/the-fix/wp/2017/01/22/kellyanne-conway-says-donald-trumps-team-has-alternate-facts-which-pretty-much-says-it-all/?utm_term=.ce947dd93c33

90 Shearer, Elsa & Gottfried, Jeffery (7 September 2017) "News Use Across Social Media Platforms 2017" *Pew Research Center* http://www.journalism.org/2017/09/07/news-use-across-social-media-platforms-2017/

91 Pariser, Eli (2012) "The Filter Bubble: How the New Personalized Web Is Changing What We Read and How We Think" *Penguin Press*, New York.

92 Mitchell, Amy (7 July 2016) "Key findings on the traits and habits of the modern news consumer" *Pew Research Center*. http://www.pewresearch.org/fact-tank/2016/07/07/modern-news-consumer/

93 Johnson, Jenna & Gold, Matea (17 February 2017) " Trump calls the media 'the enemy of the American People.' " *The Washington Post*. https://www.washingtonpost.com/news/post-politics/wp/2017/02/17/trump-calls-the-media-the-enemy-of-the-american-people/?utm_term=.42f22337c542

94 Zuckerberg, Mark (16 February 2017) "Building Global Community" Facebook post. https://www.facebook.com/notes/mark-zuckerberg/building-global-community/10154544292806634/

95 Levy, Stephen (16 February 2017)) "Behind the Scenes of Mark Zuckerberg's Manifesto." *Wired.* https://www.wired.com/2017/02/behind-the-scenes-of-mark-zuckerbergs-manifesto/

96 Fletcher, Richard & Kleis Nielsen, Rasmus (21 June 2017). "Using social media appears to diversify your news diet, not narrow it" *Nieman Lab.* http://www.niemanlab.org/2017/06/using-social-media-appears-to-diversify-your-news-diet-not-narrow-it

97 Pariser, Eli (7 May 2015) "Did Facebook's big new study kill my filter bubble thesis?" *Backchannel. https://backchannel.com/facebook-published-a-big-new-study-on-the-filter-bubble-here-s-what-it-says-ef31a292da95#.y3lff4h9l*

98 Hosanagar, Kartik; Fleder, Daniel; Lee, Dokyun and Buja, Andreas (2014) "Will the Global Village Fracture Into Tribes? Recommender Systems and Their Effects on Consumer Fragmentation" *Management Science,* 40 (4), http://papers.ssrn.com/sol3/papers.cfm?abstract_id=1321962

99 Pariser, Eli (2011) "Beware online 'filter bubbles'"[speech] *TED TALKS.* https://www.ted.com/talks/eli_pariser_beware_online_filter_bubbles

100 Shadloo, Farshad, Head of Communications and Public Affairs for Sweden and Finland *Google.* Email interview September 2, 2016.

101 "Karin," programmer at *Google Search.* Email interview September 8, 2016.

102 "Karin," programmer at *Google Search.* Interview September 8, 2016.

103 Dutton, William & Reisdorf, Bianca et al. (2017) "Search and Politics: The Uses and Impacts of Search in Britain, France, Germany, Italy, Poland, Spain, and the United States" Michigan State University. https://papers.ssrn.com/sol3/papers.cfm?abstract_id=2960697

104 Ibid.

Published by United Stories Publishing,
Stockholm, Sweden

Copyright (c) Per Grankvist 2018

The moral right of the copyright holder has been asserted.

Printed in the USA by Lightning Source, Tennessee

United Stories Publishing is committed to
a sustainable future for our planet. This book is made
from paper from responsible sources.

ISBN: 978-9-163-95990-5

Lightning Source UK Ltd.
Milton Keynes UK
UKHW02f1848230418
321523UK00046B/2132/P